DONALD BARTHELME'S FICTION

CHARLES MOLESWORTH

DONALD BARTHELME'S FICTION

THE IRONIST SAVED FROM DROWNING

A LITERARY FRONTIERS EDITION

UNIVERSITY OF MISSOURI PRESS

COLUMBIA & LONDON, 1982

FOR JOE McELROY—
MASTER FICTIONIST

COPYRIGHT © 1982 by
The Curators of the University of Missouri
University of Missouri Press, Columbia, Missouri 65211
Library of Congress Catalog Card Number 81-69833
Printed and bound in the United States of America

Library of Congress Cataloging in Publication Data

Molesworth, Charles, 1941–
  Donald Barthelme's fiction.

  (A Literary frontiers edition)
  1. Barthelme, Donald—Criticism and interpretation. I. Title. II. Series.
PS3552.A76Z77   1982   813'.54   81–69833
ISBN 0–8262–0338–8   AACR2

  Acknowledgment is given to Farrar, Straus & Giroux, Inc. for their
kind permission to reprint portions of the following books by Donald
Barthelme: *Unspeakable Practices, Unnatural Acts,* copyright © 1968;
City Life, copyright © 1970; *Sadness,* copyright © 1972; and *Amateurs,*
copyright © 1976 by Farrar, Straus & Giroux, Inc.

ST

CONTENTS

I. Introduction, 1

II. The Short Story as the Form of Forms, 10

III. Parody as the Misrepresentation
of Representation, 43

IV. Conclusion, 80

BOOKS BY DONALD BARTHELME

COLLECTIONS OF SHORT STORIES

Come Back, Dr. Caligari (1964)
Unspeakable Pratices, Unnatural Acts (1968)
City Life (1970)
Sadness (1972)
Amateurs (1976)
Great Days (1979)

NOVELS

Snow White (1967)
The Dead Father (1975)

NONFICTION

Guilty Pleasures (1974)

In 1981, Barthelme published *Sixty Stories*, which included a selection of stories from the previous six collections, two pieces from *Guilty Pleasures*, an excerpt from *The Dead Father*, and nine previously uncollected stories.

I. INTRODUCTION

Let's begin with the midden heap. Flip through a lengthy bibliography of Donald Barthelme's work and you will find a small but arresting category: "Publicly Disavowed Forgeries of Stories Allegedly Written by 'Donald Barthelme.' "[1] As in one of his own stories, what we have here are authenticated examples of fake objects, truly false fictions. The idea of a parody of a writer whose speciality is parody intrigues me. What might Barthelme have felt when he first discovered these publications? Perhaps outrage and pride, a pair of canceling emotions. The content, and the structure, of many of Barthelme's stories is built out of the junk, the refuse of our culture, our post-Gutenberg heap. And here the very success of an innovative style has become the cause of yet more imitation, more spurious reproductions, which in turn have to be properly identified. A parody of parodies is indeed an irony of ironies. But is it a final triumph or a conclusive failure for fiction to copy copies of copies?

Barthelme's fiction raises many of the questions that plague current literary theory and that seem to be involved in a fitful but widespread feeling of cultural crises. Is there a stable subject, an authorial identity that anchors meaning and intention, or is writing a transpersonal process so involved with models and transgression of models as to be completely without stable reference, let alone verisimilitude? We can easily enough identify Barthelme as a writer of metafiction (I choose this term over other contenders such as *surfiction* and the *new fiction*), as one who writes less obviously about the traditional subjects—love, fame, death—than about the conventions of writing itself. But this easily made identification can serve to blur other issues,

---

1. See *Donald Barthelme: A Comprehensive Bibliography and an Annotated Secondary Checklist*, ed. Jerome Klinkowitz et al. (Hamden, Conn.: Archon Books, 1977), p. 123.

issues that have been drawn up by opposing camps and have more or less calcified in the last twenty years or so. Art should deal with life, with ethical values, with people's felt needs and shared experiences, and do so in a common language and with conventional means. So says the traditional camp. No, says the innovative side, fiction's first duty is to show us ourselves; and since we have so utterly changed, in order for fiction to be true or even dutiful, it must also be changed. The problem could easily be transformed into a question of deciding if we have indeed changed, and if so, in what ways. But to pose the question that way is to become too general, too "extraliterary," too far removed from fiction itself. The problem then will be addressed in and through fiction: this is about the only thing on which the two camps agree.

But even here there may be dissent. Some people argue that Barthelme's work is not fully serious and won't help—negatively or positively—to clarify the problem. For some, Barthelme's fictions are too often "like the blowing of dandelion fluff: an inconsequential but not unpleasant way of passing the time." Yet for others the stories have something like a moral purpose, "to detach us from things, possessions, conventional urgencies."[2] To deal with junk, refuse, fragments is obviously an ambiguous undertaking. It will always strike some as inconsequential, basically unserious, while others will see it as somehow apposite or even restorative in a culture like ours that seems obsessed with production for its own sake. Those things that are in the Emersonian saddle and that ride us so relentlessly have to be dealt with in some way, even when, or especially when, they wear out, break down, and are discarded. To quote another American thinker: William James said that wisdom is knowing what to overlook. In this context Barthelme may appear unable to ignore what has already been stamped as ignorable, wasted, cast out of sight. But maybe he is like a

2. The first quotation is from Robert Towers, *New York Review of Books*, 25 January 1979, p. 15, and the second is from Denis Donoghue, *Saturday Review*, 3 March 1979, p. 50. Both men are reviewing *Great Days*.

holy fool, who finds things redemptive in what has for everyone else become disposable.

In either case, it is clear that Barthelme's work merits attention. Nearly four dozen essays on his work are listed in the bibliography, and some are quite discriminating.[3] His books are reviewed regularly and widely, his name is often mentioned, even "linked," with those of Barth, Vonnegut, Pynchon, and Borges. There is even something like a popular following for his work, based on frequent appearances in *The New Yorker*. It could be argued that Barthelme is that rarest of birds in American culture: a successful innovator. He yields little or nothing to most people's sense of the conventional short story, and his work has if anything gotten more innovative throughout the six collections of stories he's published since 1964.[4] This study will concentrate on the short stories, making only occasional references to his two novels (which are in style and matter very similar to the stories), and his one collection of "nonfiction" pieces, *Guilty Pleasures*.

A critic has suggested, given the overwhelming sense of historical belatedness that infuses the consciousness of many modern writers, that the artist has essentially two options: employ the method of pastiche or collage or else develop a severe, even idiosyncratic, form of totalization. Clearly Barthelme has chosen the former method. His tales almost always present the reader with an abundance of references to everyday objects, lists of brand names or articles of daily use or bizarre purposes, all of which contribute to the sense of the stories being pasted together out of random materials. There is also an obvious mixing of styles:

3. I can especially recommend "Barthelme Unfair to Kierkegaard: Some Thoughts on Modern and Postmodern Irony," by Alan Wilde, *Boundary 2* 5:1 (Fall 1976): 45–70.

4. Barthelme's stories exist in several formats: their original magazine appearances, the trade book, the paperback editions, and, scheduled to appear in late 1981, a collection entitled *Sixty Stories* (G.P. Putnam's, New York). This collects several stories from each of the previous collections, plus nine uncollected pieces. However, all the stories I discuss in detail, with the exception of the story about Paul Klee, are reprinted in *Sixty Stories*.

high, low, melodramatic, burlesque. Further, the structure of the stories is often a collage of elements: surreal passages alternate with humdrum "media" items, archaic fictional devices are joined with seemingly recondite forms and gimmicks. Very often details of a quirky sort might be recognized as historically or scientifically accurate. When Barthelme cites the title of a book, or the name of some expert in a remote field, or a historical event that challenges our sense of probability, he is often inserting genuine "stuff" into his stories. And his parodic use of motifs and structures clearly exhibits a thorough knowledge of literary history. Judged as reflections of their author's being "in the know," these stories are highly sophisticated cultural objects.

Yet their sophistication often seems in the service of anti-cultural impulses. The tone of the stories, as I will argue later, is mixed predominantly out of the sardonic and the naive. There is little overt sense that Barthelme wants to engage psychological or social questions of great import in a manner of high seriousness. He is first and last a comic writer. But like many comedians, he never allows himself to surrender that distinct note of melancholy. Consider for a moment some of his titles. *Come Back, Dr. Caligari* (1964): we can hear the echo of a melodramatic Hollywood movie ("Come Back, Little Sheba") and an important European classic ("The Cabinet of Dr. Caligari"). At the same time we detect a plangency, a longing for the past and the preterite, the "passed over." But the irony of the two movies being conjoined strongly suggests not real emotion, but a stylized, affected, even superficial attitude toward cultural objects. It's as if the movies offer us everything but tell us nothing. Other titles are simpler, but equally suggestive for Barthelme's sensibility. *Sadness* (1972) and *City Life* (1970) convey a key tonal element and a central subject matter in Barthelme's work, and together they add up to that specially modern psychological configuration we call "anomie." And in the background we hear faint echoes of Baudelaire's *Paris Spleen. Unspeakable Practices, Unnatural Acts* (1968), given the pervasive irony, suggests less an anthropological

4

revelation than a sardonic comment on cultural relativism, in which the "modern" is shown to be less rationally coherent than the "primitive." *Amateurs* (1976) names the group of men and women who make up the dramatis personae, characters of ineluctable innocence whose strivings for professional *savoir faire* are the focus of Barthelme's jibes. And *Great Days* (1979) hearkens back to an earlier freedom from guilt and anxiety, or ahead to some improbable utopia drawn up out of the deepest psychological needs and the shallowest cultural artifacts.

In an early story called "Me and Miss Mandible," from his first collection, *Come Back, Dr. Caligari*, Barthelme demonstrates his manner and his concerns. The story is told by a narrator who claims to be thirty-five, a former insurance claims adjuster and army veteran. Yet his situation has developed out of a mistaken notion that he is only eleven. The authorities are hopelessly stupid and fail to recognize their mistake and so have assigned him to a grade school class run by Miss Mandible. She harbors an erotic longing for the narrator, who in turn is obsessed with Sue Ann Brownly. "Although between eleven and eleven and a half," Sue Ann "is clearly a woman, with a woman's disguised aggression and a woman's peculiar contradictions." The story is told in the form of about two dozen dated diary entries that generate comic and pathetic confusions that result from, and contribute to, the narrator's dilemma. What makes the story funny is that Barthelme skillfully uses the device to insure that either possibility is plausible, though impossible: a precocious eleven-year-old has all the awareness and self-consciousness of a grown man in a hideous bureaucratic trap; or a thirty-five-year-old is clearly but consistently deranged enough to imagine with great detail that he has been reassigned to the fifth grade. The story parodies several things: precocious children, the bureaucracy of the public schools, sexual hypocrisy, the border between adolescence and maturity, the army, insurance companies, and so forth.

But the story doesn't create the sense that it's a serious

satire. The putative objects of its satire have all been attacked before, and few people amused by the story will be surprised or challenged by its put-down of bureaucratic stupidity or megalomania. In fact the story is less a put-down than a takeoff. Not simply an attack or negative evaluation, the story delights in a sense of play and even buffoonery. However, its playfulness derives in part from its being able to echo other, more serious forms. For example, the narrator's legitimizing prototype might be the sociopath of *Notes from the Underground* or the highly sensitive adolescent of *A Portrait of the Artist as a Young Man*, both books that use a diary format and a narrator we must "read" ironically. But the story also gently parodies (perhaps not so gently for some) the voice of Salinger's Holden Caufield. And the situation can also be read as a parody of Humbert Humbert from *Lolita*, considering the innocent nymphet and the desirous older woman. So whatever valuation we put on the narrator's tone, whether it is sheer self-delusion, but naive, or it is calculating and sardonic, we have also to "read" the author's attitudes to his prototypes.

What makes such a valuation even trickier is that the story has concerns that are part of the modernist legacy of ethical and aesthetic questions. These questions involve the problem of language, the transvaluation of values, the reflection of social disorder in the individual psyche, and so forth. Is the story possibly a covert attack on the "high modernist mode" itself? Is the story a ludic dismissal of cultural seriousness, or is it recontaining serious modernist concerns in a parodic form? In brief, is it modern or postmodern? One way we usually begin to answer such questions is to try and fix the level of self-consciousness in the fiction. But what if the narrator's seriousness is at odds with his character's or vice versa? Using a deranged, ludicrous character to advance and even criticize the author's serious concerns is of course not a new or exclusively modern strategy. (In one sense the character's prototype is Quixote.) But presenting the very opposite possibility—a serious character standing in for an essentially playful author—and then conflating the two alternative readings, this comes close to a complexity we identify as modern, or even post-modern.

The character has several serious things to say about his situation, especially about themes that will serve to focus the present study. He raises, for example, the question of cultural junk. He says his position as an insurance claims adjuster compelled him:

> ...to spend my time amid the debris of our civilization: rumpled fenders, roofless sheds, gutted warehouses, smashed arms and legs. After ten years of this one has a tendency to see the world as a vast junkyard, looking at a man and seeing only his (potentially) mangled parts. . . . I was aware that there might well be some kind of advantage to be gained from what seemed a disaster. The role of The Adjuster teaches one much.

Is this a covert, allegorical description of Barthelme's aesthetic? Certainly the attitude it describes can be traced in all the stories that follow in the twenty years or so since this first appeared. Yet what is the "much" that the narrator is taught? To make the best out of the broken? To get the best possible deal in what is essentially a litigious squabbling over the results of destiny's bad jokes? In the story the narrator actually believes he's been dismissed by the insurance company for being too fair to a claimant. Is this self-serving paranoia or the honest truth of the matter? The story's parodic structure virtually precludes an unequivocal answer and makes any answer at all difficult to assess.

Then there is the question of representation. The whole business of language and its presumed ability to represent a world for us, and us to the world and each other, is of course part of what the tradition of absurdist literature brings into question. The most radical of ironies is part of Barthelme's aesthetic. What is meant here is not that we mean different-ly from what we say, but that since we can never mean what we say (or the converse), irony is endemic, universal, a given. And his narrator has another lesson to share with us (Is his eagerness to formulate lessons a sign of his seriousness or his mania?). This one he learns from the grade school:

> All of us, Miss Mandible, Sue Ann, myself, Brenda, Mr. Goodykind, still believe that the American flag betokens a kind of general righteousness.
> But I say, looking about me in this incubator of future citizens, that signs are signs, and that some of them are lies. This is the great discovery of my time here.

Perhaps not even the most advanced semiotician can say much more than "signs are signs, and that some of them are lies." But if the "great discovery" is true, what of the great lesson of being an adjuster? Can the two be mediated? Isn't it in fact true that the flag betokens a "kind of general righteousness," though not a kind of absolute right? How aware is the narrator of his word choices? Is he a holy fool or just a comic character?

These two passages from "Me and Miss Mandible" can serve as introductions to the two main themes that follow. The first chapter will investigate Barthelme's use of the genre of the short story, suggesting that this genre is especially rich in its use of other genres. The short story, in other words, recycles junk, snapping up the unconsidered trifles of our culture and civilization for a variety of different goals. Barthelme is first and foremost a writer of *short* stories, as none of his tales goes much beyond ten pages. But in this small scope, some large issues are raised and confronted, if not resolved. And the second chapter will deal with the problem of language, or more specifically the issue of irony. Barthelme is a parodist, a special sort of ironist, whose focus is less the gap between word and thing, or desire and object, but more that of the gap between word and word, or manifested desire and desirable manifestation. Along the way, I will raise questions about some aspects of modernism and post-modernism.[5] And I will also touch on narrative theory, asking, again in a general way, about the applicability of

5. I should record a general debt here to the work of Fredric Jameson, especially his essay, "The Ideology of the Text," in *Salmagundi* 31–32 (Fall 1975-Winter 1976): 204–46.

narrative models from earlier eras in Barthelme's thoroughly modern world.

Miss Mandible bears in her name the suggestion of destructive, aggressive action, but her name also suggests another sort of activity when we recall such phrases as "chew it over" and "endless jawing." She can, then, serve as a sort of figurehead for an attack, but also a meditative consideration, a dual activity that has analogues in both fiction and criticism. Barthelme's stories may offer us some discovery that will explain the junk and the signs, even if we have to consider the possibility that they are one and the same.

II. The Short Story as the Form of Forms

About fifty years ago, Elizabeth Bowen, in her introduction to the *Faber Book of Modern Short Stories*, compared the short story to the cinema, that other "accelerating" art form. She listed three affinities between the two:

> neither is sponsored by a tradition; both are, accordingly, free; both, still, are self-conscious, show a self-imposed discipline and regard for form; both have, to work on, immense matter—the disoriented romanticism of the age.

Such affinities may not seem very illuminating at first glance and may strike some as the result of an intuition that barely rises above the journalistic. Still, the three points are worth considering, if only as a way to orient Barthelme's talent in terms of this protean genre. Take the last point first: the immensity of matter. This is perhaps the most obvious characteristic of Barthelme's work, its heterogeneous range of subjects, or at least its range of references. The stories in some sense reflect their place of publication, namely the modern magazine. Addressed to an audience with a relatively wide experience of travel, an acute sense of fashion and change, as well as a consciousness formed in part by a purposely pliant cultural context, these stories must constantly widen, shift, and quicken their readers' sense of timely details. In a sense, Barthelme's stories must compete with, even as they ironically comment on, the advertisements and nonfiction "features" that surround them. This calls for a fictional voice that is both coy and disaffected, naively desirous and dispassionately suave, especially in regard to the vagaries of status and the quicksilver tokens of its possessors.

Which leads us to Bowen's characterization of the age's matter: a disoriented romanticism. It's easy to imagine how Barthelme would respond to such a phrase. In fact, one could imagine him writing a brief sketch or story that would revolve around the very inanity such a phrase can lend itself to. Yet it's just the tone of this phrase—an exhaustion that wants to proclaim itself, but that must be on guard against making its very lack the ground for too large a claim—that Barthelme's fiction often explores. For the typical Barthelme character, it is just the variousness of the world that spells defeat, since the variety is both a form of plenitude and the sign of its absence. The realm of brand names, historical allusions, "current events," and fashionable topics exists in a world whose fullness results from the absence of any strong hierarchical sense of values, and the casual randomness of such things both blurs and signals how any appeal to a rigorous, ordering value system would be futile.

The second affinity between the short story and the cinema suggests a similar double truthfulness. Where the immensity of matter is both a fullness and an emptiness, the self-conscious, self-imposed discipline of both forms is also a burden and a possibility. In its earliest days, the cinema turned directly to the stage for its discipline, especially its plots and characters and settings. But before long the new form had developed strict generic limits of its own. The train robbery, the last-minute rescue in the weekly serial, the gothic horror show, the costume drama: in ways large and small the cinematic vocabulary defined itself by following its own successes. At one level this was mere common sense. Chase scenes seemed a natural thing to film, and reenacting past historical epochs obviously satisfied a longing for entertainment and curiosity. The cinema found its own mimetic boundaries, often because it discovered it could create illusions. So, to quote one cynical entrepreneur, "we give 'em what they like, and they like what we give 'em." The short story, especially in its appearances in nineteenth-century magazines, obviously borrowed heavily from the parent form, the realistic novel. Increasingly, short stories began to utilize certain devices that not only worked well, but seemed to be natural extensions of its form, generic limitations turned to advantage. The elliptical opening, reliance on especially accurate dialogue, a certain use of symbolist concentration on atmosphere, and the surprise ending (refined by Joyce into an epiphany): such things would work less well in an extended narrative. So the short story slowly built up its own tradition, in part supplying what in another context Ezra Pound said "the age demanded," an "accelerated image of its own grimace."

But how much of this discipline was imposed by its creators and how much was a response to audience demands, real or supposed? Everyone knows how hard Joyce had to labor to get *Dubliners* published, and clearly some of the resistance to the stories centered on their structural innovations as well as their bleak moral tone. The trick of writing surprise endings was that they shouldn't be too surprising. By building with care toward the singular epiphanic moment, Joyce obviously challenged the generic limits. The point of all this for Barthelme is that the devices that provided for the short story's self-imposed discipline are turned into a storehouse of parodic motifs. As the would-be short-story writer in "The Dolt" says, "I've got the end but I don't have the middle." Indeed, the story inside *this* story, that Edgar, the struggling writer, has produced as part of the National Writing Examination, is a classic parody of the opening of one of those nineteenth-century novels of frustrated romanticism. It is a narrative that could easily be seen as the equivalent of painting by numbers, a rationalized assembly of preplanned parts. But the joke is that it remains essentially a narrative for a novel, not a short story. (The further joke is that Edgar can easily pass the oral part of the Examination, having become so proficient that he prepares for it by reciting the answers and asking his wife to supply the questions. Edgar has, like many of Barthelme's characters, mistaken form for substance.)

The short story's self-imposed discipline also concentrates on singularity of effect (here Poe's theory is the classic articulation), and on a brevity, almost a static sense of character development (here the essays by H. E. Bates and

12

Alberto Moravia, among others, stand out.) This almost lapidary sense of getting just the right effect in the tightest space will undoubtedly put a premium on devices, and on the self-conscious play they usually entail in an ironic age. Each of Barthelme's selections of stories is a veritable catalogue of such devices, which are often parodied and played off against one another. One of the most subversive of these devices is the unreliable narrator. In full-length novels such a device allows the reader slowly to adjust his or her moral and veridical senses, even if, as with *Gulliver's Travels*, such adjustment cannot lead to a final, singular standard. But in the short story the smaller scope makes such unreliability resemble mere prankishness. And the notoriously final sense of the short story's closure also invites a self-conscious use of narrative trickery. Where a strained ending in a novel can obviously harm the overall effect, it does not necessarily ruin it. But in a short story such closure dominates our sense of the story's structure, even its very reason for being written. And where this dominance is too strong, as with many of de Maupassant's and O. Henry's stories, we feel cheated, as if the story is merely an excuse for its ending. Such a feeling can often be caused by a variety of devices in a Barthelme story. Rather than a free, unsponsored tradition, the short story's battery of generic devices can be as bafflingly plentiful, and possibly self-defeating, as that of any other art form.

And so as for the third of Bowen's suggested affinities, that neither the short story or the cinema is sponsored by a tradition, the argument thus far has maintained nearly the opposite. In a strictly limited way, the modern short story doesn't have a clear tradition that extends in any way like the novel's. But again there is a doubleness here. For the very lack of a tradition, seen from a different vantage point, can mean that the short story has open to it a host of traditions. If there is no mainstream to the genre before the popularity of magazine stories that originated in the latter part of the nineteenth century, still there are a dozen or so tributaries that constitute a flood of possible models and sources. Again, like the cinema, the short story's pliancy makes it a veritable devourer of other artistic traditions. Here the figure of Borges is especially germane, as he extended the story into the realm of the "ficciones," impinging on and often incorporating elements of the tale, the philosophical essay, the romantic "fragment," and other popular and familiar forms. For Barthelme, the line between the short story and other genres is, of course, a prancing, erratic, subversive line even when it's most stable. The clearest evidence of this is in his volume, *Guilty Pleasures*, called his "first book of nonfiction." But many of the pieces in this book are easily compared to his stories, and he even tries to categorize them as

> . . . pieces [that] have to do with having one's coat pulled, frequently by five people in six directions. Some are brokeback fables and some are bastard reportage and some are pretexts for the pleasure of cutting up and pasting together pictures, a secret vice gone public.

The last sentence refers to several pieces that use actual photographs and line engravings, with ironic, playful captions, recalling the once popular illustrated tales designed for semiliterate audiences. And by extension it can refer to the use of collage, one of Barthelme's aesthetic devices. But the "six directions" offers the clue to how Barthelme sees the short story, namely as a genre that is overdetermined, as it were, subject to an excess of impulses and obsessions. Somehow, wonderfully, the author manages to avoid having these impulses cancel each other out. Yet the other clues in the above quotation—brokeback, bastard, pretexts—also point toward the hybrid destiny of the genre, as if in trying to vindicate its lineage the short story had first to acknowledge all the illegitimate offspring that preceded it and still haunt its memory.

One family resemblance of a majority of the pieces in *Guilty Pleasures* is the shared source of their parodic material, the mass media. This would include such "byways" as the letters-to-the-editor column and the consumers' bulletin annual. The media are also a source for much of Barthelme's

14

fiction. In a general sense, Barthelme's work can be read as an attack on the false consciousness generated by meretricious sources of information that are accepted as commonplace in the modern, technologized, urban society of mass man. This is, however, to read the stories as more morally pointed than they are intended. But in formal terms, the stories are obviously shaped to a large extent by the fascination of the abomination their author feels when faced with the media. It seems to me the stories are built with a divided consciousness that says first that all the formats of information and narrative are compromised, if not actively corrupt. The possible response is then twofold: either use these available formats since the audience is reachable by no other, or demonstrate by a parodic "de-creation" of the formats that no real binding or altering force is left to the narrative imagination in today's world.

A great many of Barthelme's stories are structured parodically on various fictional formulae and their closely related forms in the other media. This variety of formal structures reflects the absence of clear generic demarcations in modern literature, a fact that has become commonplace, as witness such "new" genres as the nonfiction novel and the new journalism. But formal diversity is such a salient fact of Barthelme's fiction that it has to be interpreted as part of his artistic vision. Consider, for example, the first seven stories in the collection, *Sadness*. The opening story is a first-person narration of a marriage that ends in divorce. The second is a manic third-person monologue, apparently addressed by a mother to her son, an aging child-prodigy. Next comes a story, called "The Genius," made up of nonsequential paragraphs, some only a sentence or two long (the story is structured much like "Robert Kennedy Saved From Drowning"). Then there's a story built out of numbered sections, but told in a relatively continuous narrative line, although the line is "split" between two major characters. (Here the characters are an estranged couple, much like the one in the first story.) The fifth story is built on the conceit conveyed by the title, "A City of Churches"; a newcomer is instructed in the rather bizarre local piety and is both repelled and entangled by the repressive forces that are symbolized by the several dozen ecclesiastical structures that dominate the city. The sixth story, "The Party," is a first-person monologue concerned with the whacky events and overheard chatter among the guests, as well as with the narrator's not-too-secure relationship with his friend, Francesca, to whom the story is ostensibly addressed. The seventh story concerns the artist Paul Klee, during his service in the German Air Force in March 1916. It is constructed out of two overlapping but partly contradictory accounts, one given by Klee himself and the other drawn from the files of the Secret Police who have the artist under surveillance.

All in all, a very mixed bag, and no two of the stories are related in terms of the effect of their formal structures. Two are told from a first-person point of view, but "The Party" is much like a manic letter or plea to Francesca, whereas the first story is told very dispassionately. The two stories that have a split focus are also quite different in effect, as are the two that are made up out of discrete paragraphs (the first using nonnumbered, nonsequential units, the other using numbers and a fairly continuous narrative line). Thematically, some of the stories can be loosely grouped: two deal with divorce or estrangement, two deal with an individual trying to manoeuvre around repressive, institutionalized forces, two have manic narrators (one first-person, the other third) who clearly suffer from paranoia, and so forth. But it is the profusion of formal inventiveness that strikes most forcefully, especially when one glances at the rest of the stories in the collection. These include one that uses line engravings, another that mimics a catechism lesson, yet another that is a letter from the narrator to his girlfriend's analyst. And in many cases the parodied form—the catechism, the letter to the analyst, the secret police files—is both thematically appropriate and at the same time undercut by the narrative.

The story about Paul Klee typifies this dual status of the trustworthiness of the stories' formal dimensions. Entitled

"Engineer-Private Paul Klee Misplaces an Aircraft between Milbertshofen and Cambrai, March 1916," thematically the story centers on the artist oppressed by institutionalized structures. An aircraft, one of the three in his care, is "misplaced," and Klee's first reaction is to sketch the loose canvas and rope that had been covering the plane. Eventually he conceals the loss of the plane and apparently goes unpunished. This ending makes a mockery of the Secret Police files, since, though the police are obviously observing him with skill and thoroughness, the discipline or punishment such observation is meant to insure never takes place. Of course part of the story's theme is that the secret files are their own justification for being, regardless of whether they bring about punishment or reward. In fact, the "voice" of the files is in many ways more sensitive, more laden with *Weltschmerz* than is Klee. As the Secret Police say:

> Omnipresence is our goal. We do not even need real omnipresence; hand-in-hand as it were, goes omniscience. And with omniscience and omnipresence, hand-in-hand-in-hand as it were, goes omnipotence. We are a three-sided waltz. However our mood is melancholy. There is a secret sigh that we sigh, secretly. We yearn to be known, acknowledged, admired even. What is the good of omnipotence if nobody knows? However that is a secret, that sorrow. Now we are everywhere.

In some ways this "voice" resembles that of the deranged narrator from some existential novel. The self-deluding consistency and the consistent self-contradiction are played off against an obviously comic distortion of formulaic language ("hand-in-hand-in-hand"). While other parts of the secret files contain the sort of information we might expect (the registration numbers of the aircraft, for example), this passage conveys the tone of existential *angst*, and further back, the conundrums of scholastic theology. Again, at this further remove, the form becomes thematically appropriate, since parodically the Secret Police are the "absent God" that haunts the modern artist. As the story ends, the Secret Police even condone Klee's falsification of the official papers to conceal the missing aircraft, and say, "We would like to embrace him as a comrade and brother but unfortunately we are not embraceable. We are secret, we exist in the shadows, the pleasure of the comradely/brotherly embrace is one of the pleasures we are denied, in our dismal service." By this time, the Police have begun to sound like the guardian spirit of a romantic knight-errant. Meanwhile, Klee tells his part of the story in rather matter-of-fact, naive language.

Of course, among the manifold ironies of this story, one central element is the presentation of a real-life, historical individual named Paul Klee through a secret file that we presume is entirely Barthelme's invention. Some readers will assume that Klee was a private in the German Air Force during March 1916 and may even have visited the towns of Milbertshofen and Cambrai mentioned in the story. This thread of verisimilitude in some ways violates the principles of realism, which generally militate against using facts about actual, specific people. And thus the device of the secret file is both part of the possibly "real" detail of the story and a sign of its impossible, even surreal, fictiveness. By having the story incorporate the formats of Klee's diary and the police files, otherwise historically reliable sources in most cases, Barthelme playfully undercuts the historicist yearnings for "real" data about "real" famous people. And by parodically reducing Klee's sensibility while increasing that of the Secret Police, Barthelme deflates the theme of those stories about the persecuted, alienated artist. In a sense, the story pretends there is a "real" record behind the stories, the received opinions; at the same time, the story obviously creates fictional records to make its points. Clearly the fictional records are less true than the "imagined" truth about alienated artists and oppressive institutions. The story, then, "de-creates" not only imaginative stories but actual police files (since the only thing "true" about these files is the melancholy self-doubt they record, a quality strictly proscribed in all actual police records).

We can for the moment reduce the formalist play of the story to a few "statements": 1) sentimental notions about alienated artists are often contradicted by the historical rec-

18

ord; 2) the historical record is made up out of rhetorical formats that often preclude certain kinds of truth from being recorded; 3) stories, which are free to mix the actual and the imagined, might lay claim to a higher truth than records, but 4) stories, if they are to be at all believable, must acknowledge their own fictiveness, although 5) if all the forms of conveying information are equally suspect, because each in its own way must answer formal demands, then the story, by its very ability to mix and violate other formats, can approach the otherwise fugitive truth. The story, that is to say, will, even more readily than the novel, acknowledge its own formal requirements by the parodic manipulation of the formats of other genres. The short story, for Barthelme, pollutes itself so that it can demystify other genres. Or to put it the other way around, it seeks to demystify other forms because it cannot claim any but a formal truth for itself. For Barthelme the highest success is not if the story strikes us as true, but rather if it shows us how it works.

All this is to apply something like Barthes's "writing degree zero" to Barthelme's playful consciousness of generic forms. For Barthelme, as for Barthes, writing can never be a pure, transparent representation of reality; it must always involve a choice among previously formed models of selection and arrangement. And neither can writing produce totally autonomous structures free of ethical forces and temporal limitations. In a real sense all writing is compromise, an attempt to mediate between apparently pure forms that claim an unequivocal truth, however limited. The short story engraves this compromise into the very lines of its fabrication. Barthes's formulation of these problems has a Marxist-existentialist cast to it, but the terms nevertheless can illumine Barthelme's situation. Barthes says:

> It is under the pressure of History and Tradition that the possible modes of writing for a given writer are established; there is a History of Writing. But this History is dual: at the very moment when general History proposes—or imposes— new problematics of the literary language, writing still re-

> mains full of the recollection of previous usage, for language
> is never innocent: words have a second-order memory which
> mysteriously persists in the midst of new meanings.[1]

This "second-order memory" often results from the use of a word, or phrase, or general vocabulary in a specific genre. Barthelme takes the generic freedom of the short story, which is also of course a generic limitation, and uses it to attack the "old" meanings. The generic limitation consists in the very absence of a strictly definable generic format, and so for Barthelme the short story is condemned, as it were, to be a parasite of other genres.

Many genres, of course, develop historically with a given outlook or ideology. In fact one well-known definition, proposed by Wellek and Warren in their *Theory of Literature*, says that genre consists of an integration of an inner form (attitude, tone, purpose) and an outer form (structure). But the short story as practised by Barthelme resembles cinema in that it appears to be an empty form that can be filled by various kinds of matter, and so not reducible to a coherent outlook. In cinema we have the newsreel, the training film, the animated short, as well as the feature film, with its full range of generic traditions. And pursuing this a step further we can borrow a notion from an early theorist of film, Sigfried Kracauer, who formulated film's chief aim as "the redemption of physical reality." This is admittedly a vague notion, but adapting it to our purposes we might venture the following: Barthelme uses the short story for the goal of "redeeming fictional consciousness." But for Barthelme, as for Kracauer, the prior act in this redemption is mimesis. By mimicking other forms, rather than by trying to "imitate" the real, by giving the reader the experience of form recaptured by form, Barthelme is, like many filmmakers, partly an archivist. He has an obvious hunger for play and manipulation that takes for its material less character and plot than the formal, one might almost say the technical, aspects of writing. This, of course, is what leads many

1. *Writing Degree Zero*, trans., Annette Lavers (New York: Hill and Wang, 1968), p. 16.

critics to dismiss his work as trivial, and the charge has a certain substance. The reader of a Barthelme story is bound to be aware of effects. But whereas other metafictionists create effects of estrangement and disorientation only eventually to re-establish a consistency on some other grounds, Barthelme is open to the charge that he disorients for the sake of disorientation.

But joined with this largely comic disorientation there is a serious sense of a hunger for the fugitive and the ephemeral, that is in turn joined with impulses that may be called archival. Barthelme's work contains an undeniable note of melancholy, and though it doesn't have the grandeur or resonance we find in writers like Borges or Beckett, this sadness still functions as a vital part of the overall effect. This longing for the fugitive, at its strongest, comes from an existential ethos, an awareness that all human desire for permanancy remains condemned to frustration, and that to institutionalize means to destroy, though *not* to do so is to face the same result. Genres are institutionalized structures on a small scale. While they represent attempts to preserve that which is undeniably fugitive, genres are fit subjects for black humor. But while they represent attempts to create what Frost called "a momentary stay against confusion," their redemption in and through another structure can be an act of homage as well.

Too much can be made out of the purely formal aspects of Barthelme's work, however. Theoretically there would have to be some ideological content in any work, no matter how ostentatiously or genuinely preoccupied with formal matters it was. This is especially true of narratives, which implicitly tell us how people have come to be the way they are and what their prospects of change and development involve. Again, the comparison with cinema provides a clue. The early cinema, especially in the hands of Eisenstein, Vertov, and the other Russian experimentors, was hailed as a revolutionary art, superbly suited to contain the message of a new social reality. This claim was based on several factors, including the need for cooperative effort in the various stages of filmmaking as well as the revelatory and gripping effect of photographic accuracy combined with the emotional charge of "moving" pictures. A similar ideological intention has been imputed to the short story by one of its masters, Frank O'Connor. For him, the short story is dominated by "the lonely voice"; it is the fiction of "the Little Man." Tracing his notion back to Turgenev's famous remark, "We all came out from under Gogol's 'Overcoat,'" O'Connor goes on to focus on a juxtaposition. O'Connor says:

> What Gogol has done so boldly and brilliantly is to take the mock-heroic character, the absurd little copying clerk, and impose his image over that of the crucified Jesus, so that even while we laugh we are filled with horror at the resemblance.[2]

Of course, Gogol's clerk is far removed from the "new man" of socialist visionaries such as Eisenstein, even assuming Gogol had the benefit of O'Connor's Christological context to enlarge his historical resonance. But the antiheroic figure does find an appropriate home in many modern and contemporary short stories. One reason is that the story allows for little extended sense of chronological development; in a story, character seems given, whereas in a novel it can appear earned or slowly uncovered or shaped by alternating or dialectical forces. And if character is given in the short story, then society, the "other" against which we recognize and evaluate the single character, is equally fixed and unyielding. In simplified Marxist terms, the Little Man may be seen as counterrevolutionary, bringing with him an ideology that posits the impossibility of social change, let alone upheaval.

Barthelme creates many characters who are closely kin with Gogol's clerk. From the narrator, either a precocious eleven-year-old or a stunted thirty-five, who is obsessed

2. O'Connor's essay can be found in *Short Story Theories*, ed. Charles May (Athens, Ohio: Ohio University Press, 1976). This collection includes many of the standard essays on the topic, including Poe's, and the ones by Bowen and Jarrell that I also cite.

with his teacher in "Me and Miss Mandible," to the would-be writer in "The Dolt," to the frustrated speaker in "And Then": All these figures, and many more like them, have difficulty dealing with social forms. Often, as in Gogol, the social forms are agencies of accreditation or certification that make consistent but impossible demands on their increasingly hapless victims. The structure of their stories is often congruent with the exposition of their situation. Very little change is depicted; the inability to act becomes the dominant theme. Origins and apocalyptic conclusions seldom occur. Even "The Balloon," from *Unspeakable Practices*, in which a forty-five-block-long balloon covers Manhattan, raises all sorts of terminal anxieties and catastrophic possibilities, but ends with this sentence:

> Removal of the balloon was easy; trailer trucks carried away the depleted fabric, which is now stored in West Virginia, awaiting some other time of unhappiness, some time, perhaps when we are angry with one another.

The juxtaposition at the end is one between an implied social disaster ("some other time of unhappiness") and a trivial personal feeling ("when we are angry with one another"). Besides Gogol's clerk, Prufrock lingers in the background here, as someone for whom eating a peach and disturbing the universe are commensurate and unthinkable possibilities.

This figure of impotence confronted by bureaucratized reality dramatizes many of the features of a society that has increasingly developed toward what Max Weber called "rationalization"—the employment of carefully chosen means for limited ends. For Weber, the domination that provides the social cohesion that allows means and ends to be mediated exists in three forms—traditional, charismatic, and rational-legal. Barthelme's fiction is clearly dominated by the third of these forms, although it has a faint nostalgia for the first and a skewed enchantment with the second. But a special sense of rational-legal forms constitutes a weird counterpart to the highly self-conscious sense of aesthetic form Barthelme constantly exhibits. Part of the irony in

Barthelme comes from just this tension: a highly skilled author is creating especially maladroit characters, that is, a writer enchanted with the manipulation of artistic constructs is constantly showing us people who are baffled and defeated by bureaucratic forms. And, again, it is the very transparency of the short story genre, its openness to other genres, that allows Barthelme access to the greatest range of forms, allusions to form, and formalized behavior.

As O'Connor puts it: "In discussions of the modern novel we have come to talk of it as the novel without a hero. In fact, the short story has never had a hero. What it has instead is a submerged population group." Add to this the feeling that for Barthelme's fiction the submerged population group has been extended to become virtually coterminous with the entire society, and you have a fair sense of what the stories are about. Barthelme's characters, for all their tics and guilts, are like flawed versions of Phillip Reiff's "therapeutic man," people hyperconscious of the mechanisms of repression and neurosis but unable effectively to alter their condition. It is this psychological literacy that also gives them access to the various forms the stories parody. In Barthelme the narrator or main character has always read the current best-seller, has always just finished a course in self-improvement (or has promised himself he will begin soon), has always learned the value of appearances. As I said earlier, the typical character values form over substance, but he is also often defeated by his inability to deal properly with form.

One story that exhibits many of these themes and characteristics is "At the End of the Mechanical Age," from *Amateurs*. Here is the opening section:

> I went to the grocery store to buy some soap. I stood for a long time before the soaps in their attractive boxes, RUB and FAB and TUB and suchlike, I couldn't decide so I closed my eyes and reached out blindly and when I opened my eyes I found her hand in mine.
>
> Her name was Mrs. Davis, she said, and TUB was best for important cleaning experiences, in her opinion. So we went to lunch at a Mexican restaurant which as it happened she

owned, she took me into the kitchen and showed me her stacks of handsome beige tortillas and the steam tables which were shiny-brite. I told her I wasn't very good with women and she said it didn't matter, few men were, and that nothing mattered, now that Jake was gone, but I would do as an interim project and sit down and have a Carta Blanca. So I sat down and had a cool Carta Blanca, God was standing in the basement reading the meters to see how much grace had been used up in the month of June. Grace is electricity, science has found, it is not *like* electricity, it *is* electricity and God was down in the basement reading the meters in His blue jump suit with the flashlight stuck in the back pocket.

"The mechanical age is drawing to a close," I said to her.

"Or has already done so," she replied.

"It was a good age," I said. "I was comfortable in it, relatively. Probably I will not enjoy the age to come quite so much. I don't like its look."

"One must be fair. We don't know yet what kind of an age the next one will be. Although I feel in my bones that it will be an age inimical to personal well-being and comfort, and that is what I like, personal well-being and comfort."

"Do you suppose there is something to be done?" I asked her.

"Huddle and cling," said Mrs. Davis. "We can huddle and cling. It will pall, of course, everything palls, in time. . ."

The God here recalls the play by Bruce Jay Friedman, in which the Supreme Being turns out to be a Puerto Rican attendant in a steambath. Barthelme's story is clearly in the absurdist tradition, for this and other reasons. But notice how the details and the run of certain sentences in the story recall other fictional forms. We can hear a quick mocking reference to the woman's magazine story in "nothing mattered, now that Jake was gone"; the tone of the first exchange of dialogue recalls, say, the fiction of John Cheever or John O'Hara, though the actual references don't fit that mode at all. The reference to grace and electricity refers to the sort of surrealism made popular by Vonnegut and Brautigan, while the phrases "interim project" and "the mechanical age" mock the jargon of academic disciplines. The conceit about electricity may have been inspired by the ironic Auden poem, "Petition," in which God is asked to send us "power and light." But the structure of the story has a further and more complex ironic resonance. The narrator and Mrs. Davis eventually marry and then divorce. But before they marry, each sings to the other a "song of great expectations." The somewhat lengthy songs are in fact parodies of a sort of epithalamion, in which an ideal mate, a Jungian *anima*, is described as coming to satisfy the deepest desires of each partner. Further back still is the ecstatic description from the *Song of Songs*, though Barthelme's hymns are thoroughly modern in content. The irony, of course, is that the two characters are not at all comparable to the ideal mates of the songs. But a further irony is generated by the actual wedding itself, which is attended by God, "with just part of his effulgence showing," and the narrator wondering "whether He was planning to bless this makeshift construct with His grace, or not." What we see finally in the story is a parody not only of the epithalamion but also the story of Genesis, and the Miltonic version of Adam and Eve's marriage from *Paradise Lost*. The new age, the post-mechanical epoch, is thus analogously linked with the post-lapsarian world. By implicit comparison the new electronic or cybernetic or post-industrial age (Barthelme doesn't name it in the story) will make the now passing mechanical age look paradisal.

At the end of the story, the narrator is in the same position as when it began, a helpless bystander blindly stabbing at a future over which he has no control but into which his air of knowingness will carry him almost protectively. (Ralph and Maude are the names of the ideal mates in the hymns, and the explanation referred to is Mrs. Davis's disquisition on how marriage is "an institution deeply enmeshed with the mechanical age.")

> After the explanation came the divorce.
> "Will you be wanting to contest the divorce?" I asked Mrs. Davis.
> "I think not," she said calmly, "although I suppose one of us should, for the fun of the thing. An uncontested divorce always seem to me contrary to the spirit of divorce."

"That is true," I said, "I have had the same feeling myself, not infrequently."

After the divorce the child was born. We named him A.F. of L. Davis and sent him to that part of Russia where people live to be one hundred and ten years old. He is living there still, probably, growing in wisdom and beauty. Then we shook hands, Mrs. Davis and I, and she set out Ralphward, and I, Maudeward, the glow of hope not yet extinguished, the fear of pall not yet triumphant, standby generators ensuring the flow of grace to all of God's creatures at the end of the mechanical age.

The joining of hands here signals separation, whereas in the opening paragraph it meant a new joining. Viewed as "generators," the characters are perfect metaphors for the period of transformation from the mechanical to the post-mechanical age, while the modifier "standby" reduces them to the realm of the superfluous. And the mixture of moods, the hope and fear, mimics the similar balance achieved in the famous last lines to *Paradise Lost*. In the largest terms, the story parodies the themes of fin-de-siècle melancholy and the uncertain hopes of the dawning of a new age, both classic literary subjects.

There are at least two ways to formulate the ideological implications of this story's structure. The first is implied in what has been said, namely, an impotent narrator confronts issues beyond his powers, though not his comprehension, and the story leaves him as immobilized by choice as it found him. His is O'Connor's "lonely voice," he is kin to Gogol's clerk, brought up to date with references to contemporarily fashionable details such as casual divorces, ethnic food, and mid-cult versions of historical theories. The second way is to see the structural play in the story as an ideological matrix, in which various versions of historical development and individual responsibility are intermingled.

Viewed in this way, the story's structure becomes a complex of impulses, some of which the author cannot make fully known, since they are so deeply inscribed in not only the original genres but also in their present layering. Take the hymns of praise each partner sings to the other. At one level they are built on the separation of gender and the stability of marriage as an institution that controls otherwise unlimited instincts. Yet the parody of the form suggests that such social controls are no longer effective. The narrator's song to Mrs. Davis paints a portrait of a man "right in the mud with the rest of us," though his mate "will be fainting with glee at the simple touch of his grave immense hand." As for Mrs. Davis's song, she presents a woman with "inhuman sagacity," Adamic powers, the ability to bestow names on things; the irony is that the song uses as its examples of such originating nomenclature a list of tools, including the needle-nose pliers, the rat-tail file, the ball-peen hammer, and so forth. Clearly the gender stereotypes are being reversed: the woman knows all about tools, while the man is charmingly ineffective in practical matters. (Barthelme is also alluding to the biblical notion of fallen man needing to earn his bread through work; at the same time he is mocking the irrelevance of such tools for the coming age.) An analogous irony is generated by the juxtaposition of the historical patterns the story presents, in which a potentially new era is shown to be no more than a repeated moment of transition, so the hope of social and cultural renewal is offset by the dislocations and ennui of the beginning of yet another epoch. The creation myth and epithalamion structures are canceled, as it were, by those of the woman's magazine story, with its emphasis on the normalization, even the rationalization, of matters of desire and self-fulfillment. The spirit of divorce (seen in so many Barthelme stories that it may be his single most recurrent subject) demands contest, and of course the rational-legal systems are meant to control this contest, though their actual function is often to prolong it.

As for the closure of the story, we have already seen how it hovers over the end of one age and the beginning of another. But other details are at issue: the child, for example, is both a symbol of stylized competition, his first name being the initials of the national federation of labor unions, while his place of exile is simultaneously suggestive of conflict (Russia) and serenity (a life expectancy of more than a century). (Recall how the balloon, in the story of that title, is stored in West Virginia. Place is always loaded with cultural significance for Barthelme, having spent much of his time in what was a cultural periphery, Houston, and the last two decades or so at the center, New York City.) Thus the surprise ending of the short-story genre is both enacted and dismissed, as the child's bizarre name and fate erupt in the story's narrative line and at the same time benignly close it. As a totally enclosing structure the story implicitly says that nothing will happen, or to put it more accurately, many different, disruptive events will occur, but the end result will be a sense of stasis. There will be recurrent modes of apocalyptic yearning, to be sure, and some actual historical and social changes will foster anxiety and ennui. But finally, whether the metaphor consists of divinely given grace or humanly engineered electricity, there can be "no exception to general ebb/flow of world juice and its concomitant psychological effects," as Mrs. Davis's explanation of marriage puts it.

Seeing the story as a dismissal of older narrative forms is to see it only from one perspective. The alternative perspective would suggest that by salvaging earlier forms, Barthelme is in fact paying homage to earlier visions. The story, after all, does have a visionary subject matter in the case of the songs of great expectations, although the vision is in no way offered as a ready or even legitimate possibility. Still, old forms are the residue of old dreams. And we might see Barthelme's surreal juxtapositions as attempts to go beyond (or beneath, or outside) the everyday superficial flux of consciousness. Because of his irony, his suspension between or among various opposing stances, at least two governing contexts are possible. First, his method of recycling is "merely" a reflection of the fragmented, disoriented, leveling value systems operating in today's society. Second, his recycling constantly offers to contemporary consciousness the detritus of the past (even the immediate past) on the assumption that the half-remembered visions will serve to keep alive some glimmer of a transcendent belief.

The first of these possibilities is perhaps the more acceptable. By his constant use of fragments, Barthelme would seem to defeat any sense of a transforming or totalizing artistic vision. To say this, however, may mean little more than that Barthelme is no Dante or Tolstoy and doesn't aspire to be. The use of fragments can be defended by saying that the contemporary writer of fiction mistrusts any attempt to totalize. Furthermore, it was the hunger of the modern masters, such as Joyce, Woolf, and Faulkner, to create a total vision that drove them into the recesses of myth and interior consciousness. To deal exclusively with surfaces in the contemporary world is to deal with fragments. And to deal with surfaces in fact constitutes an achievement of sorts, for it means the writer rejects the attractions of transcendent, totalizing systems as versions of mystification. In an interview[3] Barthelme has, however, turned the tables on any assumption that his art is built solely on fragments. The interviewer asks if Barthelme's earlier statement, "Fragments are the only form I trust," represents his aesthetic. The negative answer takes the form of a playful "public recantation" that Barthleme casts in the form of a mock newspaper item in *Women's Wear Daily*, complete with headlines, subheads, datelines. But even without this witty authorial disclaimer, I think the stories do present a vision that is not exclusively one of fragments, although the process of fragmentation—aesthetic, as well as social and psychological—is certainly a significant part of Barthelme's work.

The second alternative, that the recycling of generic matter, even in fragmented or allusive form, consciously offers a set of flawed utopian visions, must be considered. Of course, to offer visions that the containing structure implicitly identifies as partial and hence ineffective, might strike readers as aggressively antiutopian. Here we arrive at an

3. In *The New Fiction: Interviews with Innovative American Writers*, by Joe David Bellamy (Urbana, Ill.: University of Illinois Press, 1974).

impasse, an impasse that will separate the admirers of Barthelme from those who find his work superficial or affected. In a larger sense, it depends on how we read. Perhaps we use something like Northrop Frye's scheme of literature as always speaking to a vision of a classless society, an ideal community, which the species must always remember and yearn for. In this case, Barthelme will be a truly comic writer whose centripetal structures are an enactment, although one often perversely presented, of the "archetypal function of literature in visualizing the world of desire," as Frye puts it in *Anatomy of Criticism.* But if we come to stories more for a reflection of how we live now, or even more seriously as a criticism of life, Barthelme's playful use of fragments will strike us as irresponsible and ludicrous.

To put the best possible case for Barthelme would be to make something like the following argument. Any artist today, who accepts the demystified sense of a humanist vision that turns away from the comfort of a transcendent system of beliefs and values, must acknowledge the irrational and fragmented social structures that dominate our lives. But such acknowledgment need not turn into a maelstrom of existential *angst.* In fact, we can take some comfort,—albeit limited,—in knowing that humans have at least conceived transcendent schemes as part of their cultural legacy. The problem now is to create an art that disentangles those past visionary schemes from their elements of self-delusion and self-aggrandizement. At the same time, such heroic cultural ideals are not to be achieved easily, no matter if now we feel we are in a privileged position regarding our past illusions. In short, man is most human when he neither ceases to dream, nor takes his dreams at their own valuation.

Any moral formulation can have at least two differing tonal casts to it. Both Hamlet and Falstaff know that desire always outstrips capacity, though one is defeated by this awareness while the other laughs at it. For absurdists, such as Beckett, the formulation might go like this: man deludes himself with both appetite and consciousness, since neither is fully consistent in apprehending the world, and all systematic explanations will eventually fail. Yet man cannot simply stop trying to explain the world systematically, since such a longing for consistency is as inextinguishable as our appetite and our need to know. Barthelme sees this, or something like it, but sees it from a comic vantage point. For him, man, especially mass man, or little man, continuously creates forms that will rationalize his existence. These forms return to defeat him, in large part because they exclude and curtail and delimit his desires and consciousness. But rather than reject these forms as simple encumbrances, man recalls and repeats them because they reassure him that his littleness, his mass identity, is not all he has. Here Freud's *Beyond the Pleasure Principle* is obviously relevant, with its notion that the "repetition compulsion" is based on a desire to return to an earlier, simpler form of existence. I will deal with this notion later on when I discuss Barthelme's irony, especially as his sense of parody involves repetition.

But there is an ideological scheme that illumines Barthelme's comic sense of form as that which must be clung to and yet fought against. This is the sense of seriality that has been formulated by Sartre.[4] Put simply, Sartre's scheme says that men enter the social contract and surrender their individuality in order to achieve a social and historical goal. In modern history especially, this grouping eventually provides each individual with considerable freedom and self-definition. Then, however, as each individual becomes increasingly self-defining, he also tends to lose the earlier sense of collective identity. But instead of thousands, or millions, of distinct individuals, society produces men who are in effect isolated by their very individuation, so that each can no longer see the other as like himself. However, each suffers this same limitation of vision and so in fact does resemble the other; this is serialization, where everyone's

4. For a useful exposition, see Fredric Jameson, *Marxism and Form* (Princeton, N.J.: Princeton University Press, 1971), pp. 247–50. Sartre's analysis itself appears in *Critique of Dialectical Reason*.

longing for a distinct identity has the paradoxical effect of making all men virtual strangers and yet interchangeable. The group identity has been atomized, as it were, and the principles of cohesion and fraternity are dissolved. It is the phenomenon of mass man, but its development is given special clarity by Sartre's explanation of its dialectical formulation.

This strikes me as pertinent in the case of Barthelme, because of his emphasis on social forms that are intended to bridge the gap between individuals but actually only serve to exacerbate the sense of impotence caused by social atomization. Sometimes this ideology is thematically explicit. For example, in stories like "The Indian Uprising," "Marie, Marie, Hold On Tight," and "The Rise of Capitalism," social unrest has become part of the very fabric of modern urban life. But the unhappiness and longing that fuel this unrest are drained off into individualized psychological distortions. And at this level, the unrest becomes reshaped as mere personal quirks and so lacking in any real social import. Take a brief passage from "The Rise of Capitalism," in which the narrator tries to comprehend how social forces and individual identity are related:

> Darkness falls. My neighbor continues to commit suicide, once a fortnight. I have his suicides geared into my schedule because my role is to save him; once I was late and he spent two days unconscious on the floor. But now that I have understood that I have not understood capitalism, perhaps a less equivocal position toward it can be "hammered out." My daughter demands more Mr. Bubble for her bath. The shrimp boats lower their nets. A book called *Humorists of the 18th Century* is published.

The self-conscious and even self-correcting political awareness dribbles away into cliché, mundane demands, routine actions. Even suicide, paradoxically a very self-defining act, has been submitted to a scheduled containment, a rational-legal form that both defuses and prolongs it. It is possible to read the clause "continues to commit suicide, once a fortnight" as simply an exaggerated way of representing someone who contemplates or discusses his suicide often, but who never performs it, so that it has become a "regular occurrence." This is true, and many of Barthelme's bizarre formulations can be traced back to some recognizable, even plausible, mimetic referent. But we are still left with the narrator's "distortion," and it is in this matter-of-fact presentation of otherwise desparate situations that we can see the ideological implications of Barthelme's vision.

The ambiguity I have been describing—the embedding of past forms in the short story as either a submission to fragmented reality or the attempt partially to overcome it at least with the memory of some ideal—can be seen as the dramatization of the serial identity Sartre describes. In Barthelme, the individual longs for some earlier, lost cultural wholeness that is inscribed in older narrative and literary forms, with their idealizations of desire. But the inescapably fragmented social order offers only degraded forms, such as the newspaper, the advertisement, the slogan, the brand name, with which to mediate our longings and anxieties. So by using collage Barthelme can turn to the "form" that contemporary consciousness has developed for itself, and he can as an author suspend his own "affirmation" between sardonic rejection and naive nostalgia.

A digression here. What happens on the larger scale of forms such as older genres and various fictional structures also occurs on the level of the individual sentence. This is part of the very texture of Barthelme's irony; here, a few examples will suffice. Often in Barthelme's stories we run across cliché expressions of the sort that serve readers as an affirmation of shared values. To show what I mean, let me list several sentences, drawn from the pages of five different stories in *Great Days:*

— "Yes, success is everything."
— "Genuine sorrow is gold."
— "Set an example. Be clear."
— ". . . Cortes declines because he knows the small pieces of meat are human fingers.
— " . . . the unforgiving logic of this art demands we bow to Truth, when we hear it."

Each of these sentences is a cliché, a predictable, recognizable formulation, often of a piece of common wisdom. Even the fourth example, the one least clearly related to what I'm describing, has a very stylized sense to it: the knowing conquistador is obviously wary enough to spot the hideous "native practice," though he must appear insouciant in the face of barbarity. This particular cliché suggests an origin in the movies rather than in spoken axioms, but the effect is the same. This sense of formulaic sentences is counter-pointed in Barthelme by the use of surreal and collagist elements, to be sure. But one of the effects of the texture in a Barthelme story comes from this recycling of clichés and common wisdom.[5]

In these local phrases and sentences we get a distinctive mixture of tones, sardonic and naive. Clearly the author is not offering such axioms or "home truths" with the same straightforwardness we would find in a nineteenth-century author. Yet very often the character who utters such axioms is doing so out of a genuine need or belief. And so an ironic resonance is established, whereby some previous, but now clearly outdated, faith—one that used to be called a touching, simple faith—is embedded in a story where it not only doesn't avail the speaker of any immediate or practical result, but also serves to remind us how such faith is now inoperative. By falling back on such axioms, Barthelme's characters show how they desire an ethical, normative measure that will allow them to comprehend their experience. But such axioms are also part of the Weberian sense of rationalization, that cautious desire to enunciate some meaning for life as a whole that will lend credibility to specific actions. Thus, though these axioms are often uttered to cover moments of an individual's distress or ineptitude, they call up grander schemes of meaning in which vindication on a social or historical scale is at least implicitly invoked. The wisdom, the grand, shared truth has become no more than chatter.

5. Such wisdom and proverbs are part of what Barthes calls the "cultural code." See *S/Z*, trans. Richard Miller (New York: Hill and Wang, 1974), p. 205. Such widsom is to be imagined as coming from "an anonymous Book whose best model is doubtless the School Manual."

So the irony of the sentence is analogous to that operating on the level of structure. And in each case, the irony is generated by the resonance of the two tones, sardonic rejection and naive nostalgia. But in the stories this particular blend of attitudes produces a language that is virtually toneless. If the short story in Barthelme's hands is best seen as an empty form that encases the fragments of other forms, the same is also true for the "voice" that tells the stories. Another way of putting this is to see Barthelme's style as a pastiche of other styles, most of them "popular," but some more recondite. What we hear then in Barthelme is something like an anonymous voice, or to use a figure from one of the media, that amalgam of voices that confronts us as we turn the selector dial on our radio. This is how such a style is characterized by the Russian critic, M. Baxtin:

> Direct auctorial discourse is not possible in every literary period; not every period commands a style, since style presupposes the presence of authoritative points of view and authoritative, durable social evaluations. Such styleless periods either go the way of stylization or revert to extraliterary forms of narration which command a particular manner of observing and depicting the world. When there is no adequate form for an unmediated expression of an author's intentions, it becomes necessary to refract them through another's speech.[6]

The "extraliterary forms of narration" for Barthelme are the mass media; these, as well as the past forms of literary structure, serve both to conceal and to contain Barthelme's own voice. Pursuing our sense of doubleness one step further, we can say that Barthelme's own voice is both without authoritative force and yet completely in control. Hannah Arendt has suggested that in a modern bureaucratic state, since what happens is a constant shifting and displacement of authority, what we get in effect is "rule by no one." Something like this could well apply to Barthelme's style, with its curious mixture of total transparency

6. From "Discourse Typology in Prose," in *Readings in Russian Poetics*, ed. A. Matejka and Z. Pomorska (Cambridge, Mass.: M.I.T. Press, 1971), pp. 183–84.

and complete depersonalization.

Of course it is not easy to be scientifically precise about such matters, since any sense of style that would really tell us what we wanted to know would have to deal with non-quantifiable elements. Indeed, all sense of style is in large measure comparative. What I'm calling the depersonalized style in Barthelme is so only in relation to the much more affective, more emotionally charged writing of people like Norman Mailer or Joyce Carol Oates. A depersonalized prose similar to Barthelme's is found in Vonnegut or Kosinski, if by depersonalized we mean a relative absence of evaluative modifiers, emotive metaphor, and a firm sense of a subjectivized ego in either the characters or the narrative voice. What makes Barthelme's style distinctive, I would suggest, is its conjunction of a collagist technique with a relatively depersonalized texture. There is little or no intersubjective reality in Barthelme's world, at least certainly not the kind we are used to in conventional fiction. An otherwise interesting typology of fiction such as Dorrit Cohn's *Transparent Minds*, with its sense of fiction as characterized by the representation of states of mind, hardly applies to Barthelme at all.

At the same time we meet, in virtually every Barthelme story, situations and expressions that embody unmistakable emotions, most frequently anxiety, self-doubt, indecisiveness, and anomie. This is the result of Barthelme's carrying the modernist injunction to present rather than to interpret or to express, to "show" rather than to "tell," to something like a *reductio ad absurdum*. Indeed, when looked at closely, what Barthelme's style offers is a world charged with emotion and expressiveness that is constantly undercut, or displaced, or mentioned but not dealt with. Here is the opening paragraph of "The President," from *Unspeakable Practices*, which shows a typical alternation between highly subjective material and a seemingly nonconsequential set of surfaces:

> I am not altogether sympathetic to the new President. He is, certainly, a strange fellow (only forty-eight inches high at the

shoulder). But is strangeness alone enough? I spoke to Sylvia:
"Is strangeness alone enough?" "I love you," Sylvia said. I
regarded her with my warm kind eyes. "Your thumb?" I said.
One thumb was a fiasco of tiny crusted slashes. "Pop-top beer
cans," she said. "He is a *strange fellow*, all right. He has some
magic charisma which makes people—" She stopped and
began again. "When the band begins to launch into his campaign song, 'Struttin' with Some Barbecue,' I just . . . I
can't . . ."

Clearly the scarred thumb mocks what Barthes has called
"the effect of the real," the result of small details of observation that hardly advance the narrative line, and indicate
only that the contingent world is somehow behind the
story, "out there" in the flow of reality. We will look at this
"effect" more closely in the next chapter, as it is part of
Barthelme's parodic effect. But for now the thing to notice is
how the two speaking characters here reveal everything, as
it were, yet seem not to hear one another. The emotional
openness and critical awareness ("Is strangeness alone
enough?") eventually modulate into confusion and apha-
sia. And the story, and many others like it, makes it apparent that the phrase "warm kind eyes," which is repeated in
connection with the narrator's secretary, is a hollow marker, one of those numberless clichés from other stories that
Barthelme is constantly recycling. And so what might be
expected to serve as certification of the story's verisimilitude
(the pop-top cans and the scarred thumb) or its emotional
sincerity (the warm kind eyes) creates the opposite effect.

So again there is a sense of duality in Bartheleme's fiction,
in this case a sense of the hyperreal merged with the depersonalized. Another way to see this duality is to return once
more to the question of genre, and ask what, if any, social
compact exists in the case of the short story. I have already
suggested that one goal in telling stories in a contemporary
idiom may be to keep alive earlier forms of storytelling, a
redemption of fictional consciousness. This conclusion has
led to speculation about Barthelme's awareness of how
readers might recall past visions of communal or group
harmony, a nostalgia for some transcendent belief when

they confront the fallen and fragmented forms of narration so common in the media. But I have also suggested a different, opposed, readerly disposition, which was built on a notion of the story as a reflection of how we live now, and even as a critique of contemporary society and its values. These two uses of the short story, or implicit understandings of how a story ought to function, when pushed to extremes can be summarized in two terms: storytelling and information. I borrow these terms from Walter Benjamin, whose essay "The Storyteller" explores how the ancient tale is transformed into the modern story. In preliterate society, but extending down to early modern times, the tale had a different epistemological status from that of the modern short story. In part the modern short story is close, in form and detail, to such "true" accounts as we find in newspapers, magazines, and so forth, while at a far remove the tale recalls obviously apocryphal forms such as fairy tales and romance legends. Here is how Benjamin states the distinction:

> The intelligence that comes from afar—whether the spatial kind from foreign countries or the temporal kind of tradition—possessed an authority which gave it validity, even when it was not subject to verification. Information, however, lays claim to prompt verifiability. The prime requirement is that it appear "understandable in itself." Often it is no more exact than the intelligence of earlier centuries was. But while the latter was inclined to borrow from the miraculous, it is indispensible for information to sound plausible. Because of this it proves incompatible with the spirit of storytelling. If the art of storytelling has become rare, the dissemination of information has had a decisive share in this state of affairs.[7]

This characteristic of appearing "understandable in itself" would apply to Barthelme's use of clichés, as well as to the use of brand names and allusions to current events and bits of media consciousness. Barthelme's world is clearly one in which we confront all sorts of things that have only their very ordinariness to make them recognizable. The pop-top

7. *Illuminations*, ed. with an introduction by Hannah Arendt (New York: Schocken, 1969), p. 89.

can, the A. F. of L., the cool Carta Blanca, all serve as raw bits of information; they tell us the story is contemporary, that we are "in touch" enough to be able to recognize such references, and they suggest the world is swamped by its own flood of contemporaneity.

On the other hand, the bizarre, surreal references, the sudden irruptions of fantasy, and the presence of older forms of consciousness all tell us that the stories are more like ancient tales. The role of the return of the repressed in Barthelme's stories is crucial in this sense. By their very structures the stories imply that the social order and the rational-legal forms are not working. The goal of total secularization has not been achieved. Some authority, not subject to verification, and certainly not localizable, can be appealed to, however faintly. However short the President is in stature, he still "has some magic charisma which makes people—" The dash is crucial here, for it indicates how the knowing Little Man, the possessor of "information," no longer accepts the older forms of social domination and authority, yet at the same time he cannot fully dismiss them.

The stories do two things. First, they introduce us to the contemporary world, or rather reintroduce us, and so acknowledge its familiarity and make it safe. This is achieved largely by the superfluity of contemporary references. Second, they show us that the contemporary world is full of myth and fantasy, in which the structures of rationalization are constantly threatened with the irruption of unsafe and uncontainable instincts and awarenesses. This is achieved largely by the use of surreal collage and the parody of both social and aesthetic forms. This scheme of duality is reductive, however. In the actual reading of the stories at their best, these two functions overlap to such an extent that they virtually reverse themselves. It is the superfluous references to contemporary "junk" that strike us as disorienting, while the half-glimpsed bits of our cultural legacy tend to reassure us that we are, after all, only being entertained, only told a story.

I would venture a tentative bit of literary history here. The "high modernist mode" was built on at least two principles: it distrusted the positivism of the scientific world view that dominated the nineteenth century, and it also distrusted the smug moral certitude it identified with the figure of the Victorian sage. From these two principles flowed several various mediations, from Joyce's use of myth to redeem the everyday, to the rigorous phenomenalism of the imagist movement. But the disinterested Flaubertian "eye" suspended above the confusions of subjectivity, yet accurately recording the data and effects of that subjectivity, was certainly one of the dominant stylistic responses to the modernist dilemma. As Susan Sontag put it, two of the chief elements of modernism are homosexual aesthetic irony and Jewish moral seriousness. Now for Barthelme it is impossible to reduplicate the achievements of the high modernist mode. But neither can he dismiss the principles. (Barthelme speaks in his interview about growing up in the house his father, an architect in the modernist mode, designed: "It was wonderful to live in but strange to see on the Texas prairie.") As a result the emphasis on detachment and the use of collage continue to play a large part in his style. But in the meantime the cultural dislocations of the first two decades of the twentieth century have been followed by the even greater dislocations of the Second World War, the atomic bomb, the Cold War, and so forth. In brief, dislocation has become the order of the day. What had seemed at first like a total decay of cultural and social values had, by 1960, begun to be recontained in a new mode of consciousness. Instead of the leveling of values being perceived as a threat, it is enshrined by Pop Art. Instead of psychological fragmentation being treated as an affliction, it becomes commodified, with the help of the mass media, as a series of new "life styles." Instead of the new status of women, for example, being felt as a social upheaval, it becomes grist for the mills of the media.

But all this change, this sense of "the tradition of the new," has by now settled into a duality of its own, built out of change and integration, and hence a stable duality. From the vulgarization of a work like Alvin Toffler's *Future Shock*, to the redoubled, circuitized consciousness of McLuhan's *Understanding Media* to the sense of crisis in writers such as Norman O. Brown, what emerges is an awareness that some new consciousness is awaiting its answering form to give it full artistic life. Whatever else this form will express, it must be prepared to accept change, even accelerating change, as just another component of our cultural matrix, without special value or moment. Here the interest in such things as video, conceptual art, environmental art, as well as the quick commodification and exhaustion of these forms, is germane. The answering form that is sometimes suggested—as in the widespread acceptance of the poetry of John Ashbery, for instance (a writer Barthelme praises highly), and the drama of Robert Wilson—is a form that perfectly balances, and hence effectively overcomes, the twin demands of total empathy and total control. And Barthelme can be seen as part of this new sensibility, with his modernist use of collage and his post-modern sense of parody. And I would suggest that it is his use of generic awareness, simultaneously to acknowledge the death of genre and to point the way to its recreation in new terms, that makes him such a successful innovator.

III. PARODY AS THE MISREPRESENTATION OF REPRESENTATION

One of the central points of current literary theory, especially as it concerns narrative structure, maintains that general notions about realism need to be reformulated. No longer should we accept realism as natural or given. Like other styles, realism works because of a variety of technical devices, an established tradition, a canon of valued works, and a stable writer-reader contract. It is not true that realism is central, and that other styles or modes, such as surrealism or gothic or science fiction, are variations on a central style. Indeed there are even several realisms, ranging from the psychological realism of Dostoyevsky to the ironic realism of Philip Roth. Such assumptions and formulations have in fact become commonplaces among many literary critics today. Still, for many readers, even those in academic settings, the realist novel of the nineteenth century—the novel of Dickens, Eliot, Balzac and Tolstoy—is still *the* novel. In few other places in our culture is the gap wider than here. Perhaps the only similar situation, where an audience and the experts differed so radically in their assumptions and their habits of attention, was the introduction of modernist abstract painting in the first half of the twentieth century. Through a long struggle, abstract painting is now generally regarded as high art, capable of the fullest and most serious forms of expression. But there persists the charge, made by Tom Wolfe in *The Painted Word*, that only a few thousand people were ever interested in modernism. Therefore, is the triumph of abstraction the result of a redefinition of the aesthetic compact in our society, or just the result of the docility of museum goers and the hard sell of curators and critics? In the same respect, do people read metafiction because it speaks urgently to the conditions and experiences of their lives, or do they read it simply because it is valued as new and daring?

These are not easy questions, and if nothing else they show us how relatively undeveloped is the field of socioaesthetics. Virtually all artists can talk for hours about the audience, its real needs, its frustrations, its deprivations, its habits, but few can point to any conclusive evidence for what they have to say. All of this applies as well to the question of irony. The trouble, if that is the right word, with irony is that it has become so central to the modernist temperament that it's hard for many to see that it is not necessarily a natural part of literature. A friend once remarked to me that if he couldn't use irony he didn't think he would have anything to say. Such a situation makes it difficult to assess the different forms of irony, and also to measure just what new sorts of irony are being used, if any. We know, or think we know, what irony is, just as we know what realism is. And even if we don't know exactly what it is, we still know that it's necessary.

For Barthelme, these difficulties are compounded by his use of parody, a special kind of irony. Parody begins in literature, however, without any special ironic edge. Strictly defined, it means the use of an accepted format or structure for a different content from one it is usually associated with. In this narrow sense, the use of religious imagery in a love poem, or erotic metaphors in a religious poem, as was the practice of several poets in the seventeenth century, was parodic. Also, one might even call *Paradise Lost* an example of parody, with its Greco-Roman epical format and its Judeo-Christian content. In such cases parody possesses an element of celebration, for it implicitly pays homage to the esthetic appeal of some structure. But increasingly the word came to mean a special form of adaptation—or maladaptation—that had essentially comic or even burlesque intentions. Parody in this sense has always had an aggressive edge to it, an element of mockery that lent itself to satire and invective. For many readers have to think twice before they can recall an example of gentle, let alone positive, parody, just as they don't usually think of irony without it containing some element of mockery or condescension. And when what is being parodied is not a simple belief or characteristic, but instead a literary structure, the question of just what, and how, the author intends becomes nettlesome.

Parody generally has the characteristics ascribed to irony. To take one well-known definition,[1] irony has three components. There must be a double layer of meaning; there must be some opposition between the layers; and there must be some element of innocence, that is, an unawares victim or a point of view that pretends to some unawareness. For parody we have to add and modify somewhat. The two "layers" of meaning are replaced by the two structures, or the two contents, the one actually present, the other virtually so. The innocence comes about, in the simplest of cases, from the parodied style being unwittingly misappropriated. Thus, were one to parody an Anglican sermon, say, the particular style markers of that structure would still signal to some "innocent" reader or listener the expected meanings. Parody, then, is a quoting of certain styles of representation. All this is easy enough to see. But with Barthelme what happens is more difficult to fix. The parodied structure—the police file, the epithalamion hymn, the clichéd movie scene—can be used in the story for both positive and negative ends. The structure might be mocked and celebrated at the same time. All generic works, to a greater or lesser extent, use something like parody whenever they refer back to a prototype. This is why a highly stylized genre like pastoral lends itself to parody that can be conscious or unconscious, for the "appropriate" content in pastoral tends to shift, from pure escapism to veiled political commentary, for example. As for the "innocence" involved, for parody to work at all the reader must innocently accept at least the possibility that the parodied structure was once compelling. Otherwise parody turns into burlesque or mere travesty. Parody, as Barthelme uses it, is a mocking irony that is still entranced by the possibility of innocence. Yet

1. D.C. Muecke, *The Compass of Irony* (London: Methuen, 1969), pp. 19–20.

clearly the innocent structure is knowingly dealt with.

So in terms of the innocence of one of the structures, and the opposition of the two structures, Barthelme's parody does not easily sort itself out. Both structures might be innocent and knowingly used, and to some extent there may be an opposition but also a parallel between them. Here the police file and the artist's diary in the Paul Klee story as well as the creation myth and the woman's magazine story in "At the End of the Mechanical Age" are examples of this unclear status. To further complicate matters, in Barthelme's stories there are often more than two layers; in other words, there is seldom a single clearly parodied structure or content against which a "straight" or serious counterpart is being set. One of the story's structures may well parody the other or vice versa. The story becomes a field of free-floating parody, where no anchoring content or style serves as the central vehicle of intention against which the other structures are judged or interpreted. As is the case in highly complex irony such as Kierkegaard's, the ironic voice can itself be ironized, so in Barthelme the parodic center is itself parodied. What Barthelme offers, and what either misleads or angers his critics and detractors is his "unstable irony,"[2] or a parody without a clearly established ironic context. In Barthelme what we have is a misrepresenting of the mechanics of representation.

In large measure this absence of a center results from Barthelme's chief stylistic device, namely collage. By pasting together two or more styles or structures or parts of a style (Barthelme often uses imagery or diction associated with a style without employing the style's other markers), he is able to create a decentered structure of his own. In the simplest terms, we cannot say which style or structure is the container and which is the contained. Instead we have a self-supporting (or to be negative, a self-canceling) structure. At the structural level this is somewhat analogous to the self-referential contradiction of the classic conundrum

2. See Wayne Booth, *A Rhetoric of Irony* (Chicago: University of Chicago Press, 1974), where such irony is implicitly disvalued.

of the man from Crete who maintains all Cretans are liars. We do not have any way of knowing for sure which structure, or even which tone, is the controlling one in many Barthelme stories.[3] And the overall effect of this heightens, and in turn is caused by, a feeling of the author's lack of responsibility.

One way to measure such a decentered sense of the author's intentions may be to contrast it with an example of more traditional irony. Here is a poem that most readers would readily interpret as ironic, though the difficulties involved are greater than usually acknowledged. It is Robert Frost's "Neither Out Far Nor In Deep."

> The people along the sand
> All turn and look one way.
> They turn their back on the land.
> They look at the sea all day.
>
> As long as it takes to pass
> A ship keeps raising its hull;
> The wetter ground like glass
> Reflects a standing gull.
>
> The land may vary more;
> But wherever the truth may be—
> The water comes ashore,
> And the people look at the sea.
>
> They cannot look out far.
> They cannot look in deep.
> But when was that ever a bar
> To any watch they keep?

Briefly, an ironic reading of this poem would say there are two layers of consciousness involved, that of the people described and of the voice that speaks the poem. There is

3. Undecidability has become a positive characteristic for some, while others claim it doesn't even exist. See, for example, Michael Riffaterre, "Interpretation and Undecidability," *New Literary History* 12:2 (Winter 1981): 227–42, where it is argued that all notions about undecidability are the result of false assumptions about literature's referentiality. If we assume not that literary works refer to some empiric reality but only to other works, then the creation of what Riffaterre calls an intertext will eliminate all cruxes of interpretation that appear to be the result of undecidability.

opposition between the two, since the speaker apparently "sees" more than the people see, and the people's view is presumably innocent in this regard. By controlling the poem's tone, especially by flattening the cadence in lines 11 through 14, the speaker implicitly evaluates the people he describes. Obviously not venturesome, they are indeed narrow-minded and routinized. Burdened with an inability (or is it their own free choice?) to conceive a visionary perspective, they unremittingly replace depth with surface and distance with proximity. Yet we know, from reading other of Frost's poems and those of other modern poets, that the presumably censorious voice often turns around to question its own values and assumptions. The people's steadiness of view can be judged either an achievement or a failure. The rhetorical question that ends the poem suggests that their steadiness of looking becomes a solidity of character. We are left to ponder how what we call either steadfast or routine is, as it were, the same phenomenon seen under different moral evaluations.

The important point, however, is that we could never "know" this poem began to question its own ironic context if we didn't have the further evidence of dozens of other Frost poems, as well as those by his contemporaries, his essays on how a poem says two things at one time, and so forth. And perhaps most important is our sense of Frost the poet, as developed in such essays as that by Lionel Trilling, that argues against the innocent, homespun view of a poet replete with simple virtues. We have, in other words, an example of what Muecke calls "covert irony," an irony not meant "to be seen but rather to be detected." And our detection must take us away from the immediate data of the poem, for nothing there can unequivocally tell us what final evaluation the speaker of the poem makes about the people he describes. I don't think it's too much to argue that this poem is as decentered, as radically ambiguous as any by Stevens or even John Ashbery. But this is true only if we can look at the text itself. As soon as we invoke some sense of intention (and Muecke maintains no irony is possible or detectable without considering intention), we turn to literary-historical and biographical constructs to give our reading some context.

But by the time Barthelme's work comes into prominence, that is in the middle to late 1960s, ideas about a decentered authorial voice,[4] or what Richard Poirier has called a "performing self," had become more acceptable. The emphasis was now on literature, or texts, which engaged the reader's interest in the very process of making sense out of words, rather than assuming the reader turned to literature for some perhaps hidden but still discoverable, stable meanings. Clearly for some people their reading habits and their set of cultural expectations had been so thoroughly grounded in modernist irony that it had become possible (even desirable) to turn irony back on itself. One way to do this was to complicate further the moral dilemmas, and the contexts for judging them, of characters who were nevertheless still fairly "stable" as aesthetic constructs. In works like Heller's *Catch-22* and Roth's *The Ghost Writer*, the play between the main character and the implied authorial perspective took irony to considerable levels of complication. But in ironic realism there is always the mimetic mode and its general allegiance to verisimilitude that anchors the reader's interpretation. A recent review[5] of Roth's latest novel can nevertheless sound a decidedly nonmimetic note when it argues, "Everything is writing." This makes Roth sound like an exponent of Barthes "écriture," in which it is the relationship between and among various

4. The secondary material on this subject has become extensive, from early studies of alienation to the latest celebration of "schizopolitics," *Anti-Oedipus*, by G. Deleuze and F. Guattari (New York: Viking Press, 1977). I have found especially clear the exposition in Leo Bersani, *A Future for Astyanax* (Boston: Little, Brown, 1976), in particular the chapter on Lautréamont and Brontë, "Desire and Metamorphosis," pp. 190–229.

5. By Edward Rothstein, in *The New York Review of Books*, 25 June 1981.

texts that involves the writer, not the relations between words and things. Yet ironic realism, no matter how complex or playful, is still realism, and it is to that heterodox tradition that Roth's mimetic art belongs.

But Barthelme's fiction often involves a parody of the realist tradition. As we saw earlier, he parodies what Barthes calls the "effect of the real" as well as the cultural code that uses axioms and proverbs to support the reader-writer contract. Another of Barthes's codes that is woven throughout the text and makes it meaningful for the reader is the one he calls the code of actions, or the proairetic code. Proairesis means a choosing, an electing of one thing over another. For Barthes this code depends on the notion of the "already-seen, already-read, already-done"; in other words, it's a form of describing actions so the reader can readily identify them as stable, known activities without having to break them down into component actions. Barthes's example is the verb *to enter*, which might be broken down into *to appear* or *to penetrate*, and these choices of meaning could of course be broken down into yet other or more narrowly conceived actions. But we understand a series of actions by knowing its name, and this name is given authority by cultural habit and linguistic possibilities. So *to enter a door* means to appear in a doorway rather than, say, to penetrate the surface of the door itself. Reading a text, especially a realist novel, is made up of thousands of such representational terms that convey a series of actions. These series are "already-done" by the time the narrative presents them, and we accept them readily—they are for us "already-seen"—because we understand the code. Otherwise the description of virtually any simple physical action might be endlessly detailed and qualified.

In a Barthelme story, this code is often parodied, completed and frustrated by turns, so that we almost recognize the characters' actions as "natural." The narrator has chosen to tell us of certain actions over the many other parts of the series of actions he is presenting, but his choice is not quite "right." Instead of a recognizable narrative logic, we get a series of gaps and discontinuities, which are felt as such because there is almost a sense of continuity in the description. Consider a passage from a story in *Unspeakable Practices*, "A Few Minutes of Waking and Sleeping," where this is especially obvious. The ostensible situation of this story shows Pia and Edward living together in Denmark, he an American exile, she presumably a Dane, and their relationship is floundering because they misunderstand one another's needs. The story is a modern romance, which we could easily see as an anti-romance; what we might expect to be humdrum has become mysterious, while the mysterious parts of their lives have become humdrum.

> Edward resisted *The Interpretation of Dreams.* He read eight novels by Anthony Powell. Pia walked down the street in Edward's blue sweater. She looked at herself in a shop window. Her hair was rotten. Pia went into the bathroom and played with her hair for one hour. Then she brushed her teeth for a bit. Her hair was still rotten. Pia sat down and began to cry. She cried for a quarter hour, without making any noise. Everything was rotten.
>
> Edward bought *Madam Cherokee's Dream Book.* Dreams in alphabetical order. If you dream of black cloth, there will be a death in the family. If you dream of scissors, a birth. Edward and Pia saw three films by Jean-Luc Godard. The landlord came and asked Edward to pay Danish income tax. "But I don't make any money in Denmark," Edward said. Everything was rotten.
>
> Pia came home from the hairdresser with black varnish around her eyes.
>
> "How do you like it?"
>
> "I hate it."

Edward wants to interpret Pia's dreams, and his, but also obviously doesn't want to, for he already "knows" the dreams signal their unhappiness and a need to end their relationship. But in the passage quoted, we almost move from action to action with some sense of continuity. Edward's resistance to Freud is like Pia's dissatisfaction with her hair, her image as seen in a reflection. Both characters are trying to face, and not to face, their situation. But in having Edward buy *Madame Cherokee's Dream Book*, Barthelme is obviously parodying the impulse to interpret dreams (and also the systematic approach to dreams, as this book's alphabetical order makes clear). The folk wisdom of this dream book is juxtaposed to films by Godard, obviously requiring intrepretation of a different sort. The social marginality of Edward's existence is also revealed by the answer to the demand he pay his taxes, but the demand itself shows how impersonal systems are threatening his freedom of movement. Thus images of explanation and confusion are juxtaposed, as are images of repression and freedom (since Edward has the "freedom" of the exile and of the unemployed). The repetition of the general statement at the end of the paragraphs makes the entire passage appear homogenized (the statement also being an ironic twist of the cultural code), as if the thematic point of the events were obvious, even though the details strike us as fairly random.

Linger a moment over the series of actions involving Pia. We are told of her walking down the street and seeing herself in a shop window. This is clearly intrepretable in terms of the proairetic code. So, too, are the next two sentences, which tell of her trying to fix her hair. (Notice how we get from the city street to the bathroom without the movement being specified, yet we accept this by the terms of the code.) But then we're told she "brushed her teeth for a bit." Is this a random detail? Does it parody the "effect of the real"? Does it show Pia's concern evaporates into a humdrum routine? Or does it show her going to greater lengths to lift her spirit? In any case, it doesn't work. Then she cries. But crying soundlessly, and for fifteen minutes, are the sort of details that don't really signify anything about Pia's frame of mind we don't already know, so they seem like ironic exaggeration. When we next see her concerned with her physical appearance, she has apparently manifested her weariness by having "black varnish around her eyes," but we cannot be sure she's chosen this form of display consciously. We are told too much about Pia in one sense, and not enough about her in another. The physical actions do and do not reflect her state of mind, for the details are either too numerous or missing.

Likewise with the cultural objects. The Godard movies, the Freud, the compulsive reading: all these place Edward and Pia in a sociocultural context that helps us recognize their particular psychology. But the juxtaposition, the collage, of Madame Cherokee, the blue sweater, the black varnish, the brushing of the teeth, all these details overload the code and raise doubts about the author's desire to be intrepretable. Barthelme uses enough of the realist mode to imply that physical details are a trustworthy guide to psychological experience, but he also misuses the details in such a way as to imply that there is no trustworthy scheme of interpretation. The sudden shifts in the description of Pia's physical actions are not, we feel, part of what's being parodied, though in fact these shifts do somewhat strain the realist sense of continuity of time and space. Instead, such shifts are interpretable as part of the mimetic texture of the prose. They support, and are supported by, the sense of psychological realism sketched in through the incident of Pia's playing "with her hair for one hour." But the shifts don't obviate the presence of other, more disruptive juxtapositions. To put it plainly, the passage is consistent in neither the realist, nor the psychological realist, nor the surrealist mode, though it has elements of each. The collage of modes creates an ironic context that qualifies the validity of each, without giving priority to any. For the passage to make any sense at all we as readers have to be willing to read interpretively in each mode sometime, but in no single mode throughout. We have to know when each style of representation is being misrepresented.

But what are some of the consequences of these violations of readerly codes? A partial answer lies in a makeshift distinction. Assume for the moment that doubleness of meaning is referred to exclusively by the term ambiguity. For doubleness of feeling or affect, reserve the term ambivalence. The first consequence of Barthelme's violations is likely to be considerable ambivalence. It is difficult for the reader to direct the proper feelings toward such characters as Edward and Pia. For one thing the readerly code does is to insure a shared, known emotional valuation, from the crudest mechanical points of narrative (when should I be anxious about the character's safety?) to the subtlest notions of personal worth (does this character express him or herself truthfully, and do they deserve what happens to them as a result of their feelings?). Because the readers will need to adjust more or less continually their reactions to such characters as Barthelme presents, any ability to assume the author has a consistent emotional context will be more or less delayed. Here the contrast with the Frost poem is strongest. We assume Frost has some consistent view of the people in his poem, even if that view points to an amalgam of virtues we might usually see as distinct or even opposed. In Barthelme's case, no such assumption of consistency is possible. If Edward and Pia are truly representative or sympathetic characters they should be presented in a homogeneous fashion. If the heterogeneous presentation is an accurate reflection of their character, they are hardly to be viewed within a coherent emotional frame.

This in turn drives us to a sense of ambiguity. Barthelme, it can be argued, is really talking about the inability to "know" characters in any consistent way. The Freudian scheme is no more a guide to people's interior lives than is Madame Cherokee. Whatever physical actions they might engage in are likely not to reveal what they are thinking. Because of their social and historical marginality, the characters are not comprehensible in terms of everyday common sense. Their lives are disrupted, indeed they are models of disruption, and so the only way to "know" this is to register that disruption in all its manifold force. Barthelme's characters—and here the earlier point about their psychological literacy is important—know too much, or rather, the *way* they know themselves keeps them from any true or effective self-knowledge. For us as readers this means we are always offered and denied schemes of interpretation. This is the effect, and the cause, of Barthelme's collage, and his parody. To use the makeshift terms broadly, an absurdist like Beckett maintains the world is fundamentally ambiguous, whereas a playful surrealist like Brautigan suggests it is ambivalent. For Barthelme, it is both. His irony is a radical form of awareness and feeling. It says what we don't know can't hurt us. But since we know too much we are likely to feel too much, and so we end up numbed by something like "affective overload." His parody is a form of sentiment organized against itself.

Both parody and collage offer challenges to our ordinary sense of literary experience. Literature often proceeds on either a mimetic or expressive basis; it serves, to invoke the well-known study by M. H. Abrams, as either a mirror or a lamp. But collage is neither fully mimetic or fully expressive. By putting together parts of other wholes into a newly formed whole, collage disrupts mimesis while partly honoring it. The best example of this is the newspaper or matchbook we recognize in a Cubist painting. On the other hand, collage often works against the accepted structures of affect and feeling by insisting on sudden shifts in tone and attitude. Even if we maintain that collage thereby seeks to reproduce accurately what is in fact a jumble of feelings, we still must admit that the "ordinary" aesthetic expectations have been altered or played against.

Likewise with parody, for as we suggested earlier, parody has the ability to suggest elements of homage or travesty in its thrust of intentions. And both parody and collage operate with a sense of calculated disruption and defamilarization. Both also engage in a re-collection of material, invoking that sense of a "return of the repressed."[6] This combined sense of disruption and historical recall makes parody almost toneless. By resorting to parody,

6. An excellent article on these and related matters is Thomas Frosch, "Parody and the Contemporary Imagination," *Soundings* 56:4 (Winter 1973):371–92. I owe several of my points to Frosch, who mentions Barthelme briefly, but is mainly concerned with how parody can produce very different tonal results. He compares two parodies of the Faust legend, Mann's *Doctor Faustus* and Jarry's *The Exploits and Opinions of Doctor Faustroll, 'Pataphysician*.

Barthelme implicity admits that his own experience is not conformable to any singular style. Yet at the same time he implies that the question of style is immaterial or factitious, that our hallowed notions about the integrity of style and content are part of our disoriented romanticism. So parody has a sense of abandonment, since the artist can't possibly find the "proper" style, and a sense of disdain, because to look for the proper style would be to find oneself inevitably misled. The artist in such a situation will become a spokesman for the preterite, the passed over and forgotten, the disfunctional. This feeling is captured allegorically in another story from *Unspeakable Practices*, called "The Police Band." This is an extended conceit in which the police try to use music instead of armed force to control an unruly population. The idea doesn't work, of course, and in the last paragraph we can hear something like a veiled description of any artist whose style or approach to his sociohistorical moment is totally inappropriate.

> The Police Band was an idea of a very romantic kind. The Police Band was an idea that didn't work. When they retired the old Commissioner (our Commissioner), who it turned out had a little drug problem of his own, they didn't let us even drill anymore. We have never been used. His idea was a romantic idea, they said (right?), which was not adequate to the rage currently around in the world. Rage must be met with rage, they said. (Not in so many words.) We sit around the precinct houses, under the filthy lights, talking about our techniques. But I thought it might be good if you knew that the Department still has us. We have a good group. We still have emotion to be used. We're still here.

As with many parodists, the problem with the band is not the lack of emotion but the effective expression or application of it. And the persistence of intention is offset by the absence of an adequate usefulness, as substance is replaced by form: "We have never been used. . . . We sit around . . . talking about our techniques."

Barthelme has talked about collage in his interview with Joe David Bellamy (*The New Fiction*, pp. 51–52). His understanding of it is quite general, as shown by the initial comparison, but his focus on the "point" of collage can be related to its status as neither mimetic nor expressive.

> New York City is or can be regarded as a collage, as opposed to, say, a tribal village in which all the huts . . . are the same hut, duplicated. The point of collage is that unlike things are stuck together to make, in the best case, a new reality. This new reality, in the best case, may be or imply a comment on the other reality from which it came, and may also be much else. It's an *itself*, if it's successful: Harold Rosenberg's "anxious object," which doesn't know whether it's a work of art or a pile of junk.

Rosenberg's term is, of course, an example of a transferred epithet. Strictly speaking, it is not the object that is "anxious," but we who view it, or the artist who presents it. But this passage also suggests two further points: Barthelme's awareness of the modernist impulse to escape the "curse of mediacy," and the fact that the notion of collage is borrowed from its place in the plastic arts. The first point is very much a part of the continuation of modernism's involvement with autotelic theories of art. Many poets and fiction writers have striven for an art that would be virtually independent of reality. Frank O'Hara, to take one example, has spoken of his desire to have the poem be a thing, rather than about a thing. The older model of art as a bridge between the artist's feelings or vision and the audience's apprehension and evaluation of the views "contained" in the work is here being polemically rejected. Of course a work of art from any epoch can be taken as a thing in and of itself and seen or interpreted in purely formalistic ways without regard to any moral or social truth it might contain. Contrariwise, any modern or post-modern work can be subjected to a moral or social reading even if it claims autonomous status for itself. (This is clear from Barthelme's phrase, "may be or imply a comment on the other reality from which it came.") Clearly there is no way to insure that only post-modern works will be dealt with in a particular way. Parody, in fact, is possible because the aesthetic assumptions of one era can be applied to the work of another. So it is the polemical intent that such a rigidly autotelic theory is meant to serve.

But keeping this intent in mind, we can also consider the second point. Besides having a sense of their own nonreferential identity, Barthelme's stories are clearly indebted to the plastic arts. Plainly their use of collage and parody contribute to this feeling. Such painters as Lichtenstein and Rauschenberg work in a highly self-conscious art-historical framework in which parodies of motifs and styles are the order of the day. Barthelme's stories also have a sense of spatial form, as one story line is set inside or interwoven with another. And earlier we saw where the stories don't usually have an extended chronological dimension, being often unfoldings of a situation rather than the lengthy development of chains of successive events. Even the range of styles reminds one of a contemporary museum, where color field abstraction, pop art, photorealism, and several other styles vie for attention. Hungry for contact with reality, as their constant use of faddish and mundane allusions suggests, the stories want to be a part of the daily plentitude as well as a commentary on it.

Barthelme's stories are clearly "anxious objects," not only because they are seen by some as junk and by others as art, but also because they haven't achieved an unequivocal relation to their own use of styles and structures. In this sense, the stories are like the very objects they describe. They resemble the balloon in the story of that name; "since the meaning of the balloon could never be known absolutely, extended discussion was pointless." And of course the story goes on to discuss the balloon at some length. To use linguistic terms, the balloon is obviously an absent signified, it is a meaning toward which many signifiers point, but to which none conclusively attaches. "It was suggested that what was admired about the balloon was finally this: that it was not limited or defined." And the story's narrator, in what seems a desperate act of hermeneutics, claims the balloon is a "spontaneous autobiographical disclosure, having to do with the unease I felt at your absence, and with sexual deprivation." The balloon in this sense becomes like libido, an excess signifier, seeking to attach itself to any centered meaning, since it would otherwise convey nothing but its own amorphousness. Barthelme's stories are filled with such objects whose values as signs, or whose intelligibility as reservoirs of significance, has begun to malfunction. This is one reason the stories often resort to lists, which can be seen as attempts to "add up" or point to some overriding significance, but always end up as merely a collection of things.

In this regard Barthelme's parody seems to say that we constantly attach our longings to things only to realize that their very enclosedness renders them useless as adequate conveyors of the mutability of desire. Yet to ignore things, or worse still to be ignorant of the value they offer as markers of status and hedonic awareness, is to give oneself over to a realm of unknowable and confusing values. This double awareness of the nature of objects is described by Jean Baudrillard, whose writing has done much to explore the "society of consumption."

> Above all, [it is] legitimacy, . . . the possibility of establishing their [the middle class's] acquired situation as an intrinsic value (with respect to cultural, political, and professional life) which makes the middle classes invest in the private universe, in private property and the accumulation of objects with a dedication all the more fierce, autonomizing it all by default in trying to celebrate a victory, a true social recognition which escapes them.
>
> That is what gives objects in this "milieu" a fundamentally ambiguous status: behind their triumph as signs of social promotion they secretly proclaim (or avow) social defeat. Their proliferation, their "stylization," their organization is anchored there in a rhetoric which is . . . quite fittingly a "rhetoric of defeat."[7]

Here we can see at least an analogous relation between Rosenberg's "anxious objects" and the consumer items in advertisements in a publication like *The New Yorker*, with their emphasis on social legitimacy. (As a narrow measure of their half-acknowledged despair, recall the ad for the

7. For *A Critique of the Political Economy of the Sign*, trans. Charles Levin (St. Louis: Telos Press, 1981), p. 40.

expensive whiskey that uses the slogan, "Living Well Is The Best Revenge." But surely the unspecified grievance can never be adequately avenged, if only because it is unspecified.) In the stories, objects themselves become registers of their owners' (or would-be owners') anxiety, as the characters' hunger for reality is simultaneously objectified and frustrated.

From pop-top cans to detergents with names like "RUB and FAB and TUB" to nine novels by Anthony Powell: all the objects in Barthelme's world have a skewed relationship to their possessors. And in a sense this relationship is mirrored by the author's relation to his own fictional material. For Barthelme the collagist is neither fully expressive nor consistently mimetic in the way he treats his sources. The left over bits of narrative continuity and representation that he uses are themselves ambiguous signifiers of both victory and defeat. These bits suggest that the author is free to roam throughout the literary past, a virtual anthology without a binding, in order to pick up all sorts of styles, motifs, structures, and portions of genres. But the bits also implicitly demonstrate how no overarching stylistic homogeneity is possible given the author's sense of cultural fragmentation and belatedness. The collage thus becomes the way the ironist saves himself from drowning. The welter of cultural bits is assembled, stuck together in the hope that it will be an "itself," while all the time it signals a despair in the face of such discontinuity. "These fragments I have shored against my ruin." The line from the *Waste Land* stands as an appropriate motto for Barthelme.

But it is not only material objects that make up the saving remnants of Barthelme's world. Words are also used in the collage technique, and they often bear the marks of their status as things. This is most evident in Barthelme's recycling of clichés and stock expressions. By showing how words can be used as counters of status, and by showing them in their least transformative uses, he also shows how words and objects are similar. This, too, is another effect of his use of lists and brand names. But we can see from a passage in

Snow White (1967), the first novel Barthelme published, that this blurring between words and things is a conscious theme. He has one of the characters speak of a linguistic phenomenon, the " 'blanketing' effect of ordinary language":

> referring to . . . the part that sort of, you know, 'fills in' between the other parts. That part, the 'filling' you might say, of which the expression 'you might say' is a good example, is to me the most interesting part.

One important point to observe is that this filling is not the same thing as expletive or verboseness. Rather, considering the example of "you might say," such "filling" can serve as class markers and even signs of an individual psychology. People take on such phrases for a time, use them often, and eventually exhaust them. In some ways they are like a polished and grammatical form of slang. (The misuse of "hopefully" in recent times began as an example of this, though it's become much more entrenched than is usual for such phrases.) Barthelme has his character go on discussing this "filling," eventually comparing it to a sludgelike heaviness, which he characterizes as a "downwardness."

At the simplest level this is the language of anomie, the gummy extract of a sort of enervation that prevents fresh or specific communication. *Snow White* is a parody of the communes of the 1960s as well as an antiromance that both salvages and dismisses its fairy-tale prototype. But one of its chief themes is the inability of its characters, despite their shared mores and cultural milieu, to communicate their innermost desires. If the romance is the literary realm where wish and fact meet, then *Snow White* is an antiromance. Language difficulties, however, are not the only things that dramatize the problems the characters face. The people are also dominated by a neurotic relation to objects. One of the short chapters (they average a page or so in length) deals with the selection of a shower curtain, for example, and the social and aesthetic consequences of such a choice. But further there is the question of things in general and how to control them (the commune earns its living, as it were, by making and selling Chinese food for infants: Baby Water Chesnuts, Baby Kimchi, Baby Bean Thread). In the same chapter with the discussion of the "blanketing" effect in ordinary language, we also hear about the "trash question." Trash is increasing at such a rate that "we may very well soon reach a point where it's 100 percent." In the plant where this passage takes place, the items being manufactured are plastic buffalo humps, Barthelme's parodic way of conjoining the useless, the cheaply imitative, and the extinct all in one object. But even here the desire for social status operates: "we're in humps, right now, more really from a philosophical point of view than because we find them a great moneymaker." The bourgeois habit of concealing the mercenary impulse behind a veil of social awareness is here directly satirized, and the connection is made between objects and language:

> They [the buffalo humps] are 'trash,' and what in fact could be more useless and trashlike? It's that we want to be on the leading edge of the trash phenomenon, the everted sphere of the future, and that's why we pay particular attention, too, to those aspects of language that may be seen as a model of the trash phenomenon.

There is portrayed in Barthelme a downwardness of language as well as of objects, for even though they both represent a wished-for "leading edge," as often as not they are the signs of social entropy.

Much of the sense one gets about both objects and language in Barthelme is tied up with the strategies of metafiction. To write about the processes of writing, indeed to dramatize, thematize, and allegorize such processes, is perhaps something as old as writing itself. Even in the earliest recorded language—hierogylphs that list stores of food and supplies—there was probably a record of the records, some tablet that showed where the tabulations were stored. And so writing itself becomes in some measure objectified, and for all its unarguable qualities as a process and a dialectic, it has some of the palpable qualities of an object. One of these is its quotability, which is one of its chief means to becoming self-referential. (Notice how Barthelme uses "you might say" as an example of blanketing.) But there are more complex issues at stake in metafiction. A simple explanation of one issue is that metafiction seeks to demystify the process of writing, which is conceived of as illusionmaking. By calling attention to its own techniques, metafiction declares itself and so presumably saves the reader from the snares of verisimilitude or ecstacy.

Now probably few people have been "taken in" by novels or short stories to the extent they could no longer distinguish the real from the imagined. Still, to read a book is to handle an object, and to finish reading a book is to set that object aside and return to other activities, other objects. So the objecthood of written fiction, while far from a perfect system of illusionmaking, does nonetheless implicate stories into our otherwise "normal" activities in subtle ways. One can pack a story to carry on a trip, one can buy a book of stories, and in part this is the sort of blurring of function and definition that metafiction addresses, parodies, and even celebrates. This sense of objecthood can easily be made thematic if the work of metafiction raises questions of free will and determinism. Whether or not people have free will, most agree that objects don't. So to turn a book into an object, or rather to stress the otherwise marginal consciousness of readers that a book is a thing, an "itself," and not a voice, or a personal utterance, or real life, is to enter the realm of this endless argument about the nature of human volition and natural causality.

This aspect of metafiction has been addressed by Robert Alter.[8] He suggests that metafiction does two apparently contradictory things when it presents its characters at the same time it shows us they are projections and not autonomous or freely willing agents. First, this implicitly claims that the author can make his characters do anything, that he is in complete control of their actions and our views of them. But, secondly, this self-consciousness claims that the author

8. In *Partial Magic: The Novel as Self-Conscious Genre*, (Berkeley: University of California Press, 1975).

is only reporting what is there; by dropping the pretence of total authorial power of invention, the fiction writer becomes merely a reflector, or to apply the argument to Barthelme, a paster-up of pictures cut out of the thoroughly, indisputably real. Barthelme's stories do indeed work inside this sort of paradox. In almost all of his stories the characters appear as victims, pasteboard caricatures of social attitudes and psychological dilemmas, obviously "signs" only of their author's glibness. And yet they do reflect, and in some cases even expose, the way we live now, surrounded as they are by the confusing currents of contemporary events, fads, status symbols, life-styles, and so forth that surround us in real life. In stories like "The Balloon" and "At the End of the Mechanical Age" and "The President," the central situation of the story provides a genuine shock of recognition as we see certain typical, modern urban experiences return to us in fictional form. At one and the same time, these stories suggest that the "original" form of these experiences is both fictional (that is, mediated by some structure such as television or social gossip) and yet pressingly real (that is, we wake to it day after day and knowledge of it seems widespread and engaging to people.) This paradox stands as one of the consequences of the collage method, with its avoidance of the directly mimetic or expressive approaches. Barthelme's stories, as objects, operate in a realm neither completely objective nor completely subjective, though they implicitly claim the authority associated with both modes. They also hide behind the excuses that each mode implicitly offers: "it speaks for itself," and "I was only playing."

One way to show this is to turn to "Robert Kennedy Saved From Drowning," from *Unspeakable Practices*, one of Barthelme's best-known stories. The theme of this story remains ambiguous, but it involves in part the way a public figure is an invention of public needs and fantasies, and so the public's knowledge of such a person is always imperfect, because partial and factitious, yet perfect, because answerable and cathartic. The story creates, re-creates, and exposes a variety of presentations, using a series of short passages in which the main character, K., is shown in several situations. In the story's title a real-life, historical individual is named; throughout the story proper, he is called only K., as if a character in a Kafka novel. So from the beginning, history and fiction are conflated. The paragraphs variously try to "humanize" K., showing him at home with his children for example, and to mythologize him, by showing how he exists in the imagination of others. And both attempts are themselves subject to parody.

Here is one paragraph, in which K. can be seen as either human, because he is vulnerable, nervous, and yet witty, or inhuman, because the whole incident sounds like a press agent's gossip item.

Gallery-going

> K. enters a large gallery on Fifty-seventh Street, in the Fuller Building. His entourage includes several ladies and gentlemen. Works by a geometricist are on show. K. looks at the immense, rather theoretical paintings.
>
> "Well, at least we know he has a ruler."
>
> The group dissolves in laughter. People repeat the remark to one another, laughing.
>
> The artist, who has been standing behind a dealer, regards K. with hatred.

K.'s remark objectifies the paintings, turns them into mere exercises in construction and the use of tools (some would say the paintings invite just such a response). But then the remark itself is turned into an object of sorts as it is repeated, "passed around," serving as a marker of K.'s wit. The paragraph ends with the irruption of "genuine" emotion, but it remains concealed. In fact, the physical position of the hate-filled artist would almost suggest he is cowering, ironically enough behind the dealer who serves to publicize his work. The Fuller Building is a real building on Fifty-seventh Street, and does in fact house several galleries. The incident has been described by Barthelme (in *The New Fiction*, p. 49) as the only "real" fact in this story.

What, then, are we to make of the following item, from *The New York Times* of May 1, 1981 (about thirteen years after the Barthelme story first appeared), entitled "A Wisecrack-ing Prince Charles Tours Washington"? The item begins like this:

> Sipping orange juice, the Prince of Wales stood studying a modernistic bronze sculpture titled "Icarus" at the National Air and Space Museum.
> Finally, he turned away from the oddly misshapen work of art. "I'd love to have seen it," he remarked drily, "before it melted."

Is Barthelme ghostwriting for the House of Windsor as he once did for the president of a Texas university? Or has Prince Charles been dabbling in metafiction? This would seem to prove one point that metafictionists want to im-press on us: no matter how much artificial structure exists in a work of fiction, "real life" is equally ridden with formulae, stances, rehearsed material and borrowed motifs. Less grandly, we can at least notice that Lynn Rosellini, the reporter whose by-line appears on this item, has read enough fiction to use phrases like "remarked drily" with apparent ease. But what of the apparently parodic bits in this item, how intentional are they? Did the artist create a work for the Air and Space Museum and call it *Icarus* with any but an air of homily and moral irony directed at tech-nological pride? And did Prince Charles know the piece's title before he made his condescending remark? Yet if the artist meant such a warning against pride to those who commissioned the statue, was an abstract sculpture the best way to get his point across? And what are we to make of the overdone phrase "oddly misshapen"? Either modifier would have done, so both together can indicate anxiety on the author's part to vindicate the Prince's reaction, or perhaps it could serve as ironic exaggeration and so reflect against the Prince. (The noun in the phrase after all is "work of art," not "heap of metal" or "thing.")

What such a witticism does is to vindicate the entire situation. Otherwise we would have been left with the "simple" truth that society's leaders don't comprehend modern art, a safe enough "fact," or that their condescension toward such works expresses the otherwise guarded dismissal many people feel in the face of art that doesn't readily declare itself. Effectively the remark reaffirms the politician's or celebrity's identity as one who is baffled but who has the skill to pull through, and it expresses for us a sense of occasion in which our leaders, for a change, accurately speak for us. In either case, the fictional or the real incident, an object signifies (or attempts to signify) some complex cultural experience and the person involved dismisses the signification. But in doing so the person acts mechanically, like an object, responding to the pressures of an entourage and the "dynamics" of a situation in a manner that seems scripted. Both art work and public figure are "on show," and both play out their functions to the evident satisfaction of all viewers. It's easy to dismiss this example (and there are others like it in Barthelme, though none so pointed) by saying that reality has stylizations and fiction can, if it wishes, imitate them. But building up an aesthetic on such an easy formulation still raises questions about fiction's status. Recall Benjamin's distinction between the story as tale and the story as information. Surely the second of these two is what the newspaper example illustrates. But the Barthelme paragraph also recalls the structures of fabulation—the character called by his initial, the glowering spectator revealed at the close of the scene—in such a way as to suggest a genuinely playful exercise in tale-telling.

Alter's book also shows that self-referential fiction traces its lineage back at least to Cervantes and Sterne. If one of the functions of metafiction is to challenge or undercut realist fiction, it has failed, since realism has flourished since Sterne. But there do remain the general lineaments of realism against which metafiction is not only judged but against which it operates. A recent article,[9] besides offering a useful survey of theories of realism, suggests one chief characteristic of the highly developed realism of the later nineteenth century. Characters in such realist fiction are driven not

9. Marshall Brown, "The Logic of Realism: A Hegelian Approach," *PMLA* 96:2 (March 1981): 224–41.

only by outside, heterogeneous forces, but also by an inner necessity. Inner necessity for individual characters is revealed, even defined, by other characters' perception of them, as well as what they are in themselves. This process of revelation, which Brown calls silhouetting, presents an ordering of things that enables us to see "the individual neither dissolving into its other by the ironic play of reflections nor succumbing to forces from outside but being overmastered by something from within." What Barthelme's parody of realism suggests is that if people are overmastered by something from within, that "something" is a lack, an absence, an awareness of their own frustrated desires.

Barthelme's characters are often on the verge of dissolving into the other *and* being overmastered by outside forces, as "Robert Kennedy Saved From Drowning" exemplifies. The very structure of the story reinforces the notion that K.'s inner necessity is totally mysterious. We are forced to see him only as he is reflected in the consciousness of others, and only in reaction to outside forces. He has, in effect, no clear intersubjective reality, or at least none that allows us to see his destiny being revealed. In one paragraph called "A Friend Comments: K.'s Aloneness," we read that this "terrible loneliness . . . prevents people from getting too close to him. . . . He says something or does something that surprises you, and you realize that all along you really didn't know him at all." Then as if to illustrate this principle, the friend tells the story of K. acting as captain in a small boat beset by rough weather. The friend raised the question of whether or not the anchor would hold. And K.'s reaction is in some ways the metonymic reduction of his character: "He just looked at me. Then he said: 'Of course it will hold. That's what it's for.' " This absolute trust in things, their reliability and functionality, is a kind of Weberian rationalism in which means and ends are in perfect accord. Presumably we are to read this incident as showing how K.'s relation to people and events in general is essentially that of an absolute pragmatist, or perhaps more accurately, an *apparatchik*. Yet other paragraphs in the story portray just the opposite sort of character, for example in the "Childhood of K. as Recalled by a Former Teacher," where we are told "what was unusual about K. was his compassion. . . . I would almost say it was his strongest characteristic." The story is parodying the media-constructed biography of a celebrity—a form especially noticeable today everytime there is an assassination, an election campaign, or a national scandal—but its method of collage is suggesting something further.

The collage of viewpoints presents a jumble of cliché structures and fantasy items (e.g., "A Dream" and "He Discusses the French Writer, Poulet") which effectively parodies each and so calls into question whether our knowledge of K. (or his of himself) can ever be adequately represented. Yet at the same time the skill, the glibness of presentation in each paragraph indicates that the need to fictionalize is endemic in our society (and in human nature?). We might carry this one step further and say K.'s unknowability is necessary for the endless variety of fictions to continue. The story even suggests that the object of the fictions must be a blank, that the signified must be absent, for the necessary processes of fictionmaking to occur. In this way, K. himself becomes an "anxious object," in that he serves both as the center of all concern and the completely expressive absence. And he also serves as the source of the "blanketing effect" in language, for it is his unknowability that causes people to continue "filling in" what would otherwise be only isolated data of perception and representation.

I would suggest that K. is in many ways the paradigmatic Barthelme character. Although his story is one of the best of the entire corpus, the way he exists as a creation of parodic strategies makes him typical. At the heart of the matter, so to speak, is an ambiguity blended out of romance and anti-romance elements. As K. himself puts it, paraphrasing Poulet's description of the French author Marivaux, the character is "a pastless futureless man, born anew at every instant. . . . He is constantly surprised. He cannot predict his own reaction to events. He is constantly being *overtaken* by events. A condition of breathlessness and dazzlement surrounds him." The medieval romance hero and the Little Man of urban mass culture have merged into one person, one object. Perhaps this is the most antirealist of all of Barthelme's strategies, for this character denies the rock of linear chronology on which realist narrative erects its faith. But notice that the character is not simply an object among other objects, for in some sense he reflects, even epitomizes his environment. This reflection is one of the main characteristics of the realist hero. In fact, the syntax of the last sentence quoted is ambiguous, since we can't be sure if the dazzlement is directly the nature of the events, or if it's the character's reaction to those events that overtake him. It can be argued that the character is at one with his environment, or completely victimized by it, and this brings us back to the ambiguity of tones in Barthelme, that mixture of nostalgia and disdain. Also it recalls the mix of total freedom and total determinism brought about by the ambiguous authorial control in Barthelme's metafiction.

In large terms, there are few characters in Barthelme's fiction with distinctive psychological identities. The paradigm I have discussed is repeated often, though with clearly differing details. But this is the result of Barthelme being more "maker" than "author," more collagist than oracle or psychological realist. All the language is in his hands. This paradigmatic character tends to become identified with the author, especially for readers trained on the ironic realism of writers such as Joyce. And this confused identity of author and character takes on a profile that is distinctive, at least in its own terms. We hear this meta-voice, as it were, most clearly in the catechetical stories, built out of questions and answers. Presumably the voice is both questioner and respondent, a sort of Prufrockian split personality who can really speak most openly only when he speaks to himself. These stories occur in *City Life* ("The Explanation" and "Kierkegaard Unfair to Schlegel") and more often still in *Great Days*. They represent models of control, since the voice supplies both query and answer, but they are also investigations of compulsion and overdetermination. Speaking generally, the questioner is knowing and somewhat self-conscious, while the respondent is anxious, largely impotent, and very driven. And in several of the stories in *Great Days* the use of questions diminishes and what we get is dialogue in which claims and counterclaims, suspicions and further suspicions build up a sense of an insoluble dynamic. This is most clearly thematized in "The Leap," from *Great Days*.

This story is about Kierkegaard's leap of faith, which one speaker purposes to the other as something to be done on the day the story occurs. Of course planning such a leap is contradictory. Barthelme's irony often begins with such a broad subject, and then works variations on it. In this case the proposer and the other character (or "voice") succeed in talking each other out of taking the leap, but not before parodying several theological concepts, including the notion of "caritas" or divinely inspired love. The story reveals the characters' double-mindedness, their endemic irony that leads them both off into tangents and yet further into the implicit consequences of the topic. They finally decide to take the leap another day, and the story ends with their imagining such "another day."

> — Another day when the singing sunlight turns you every which way but loose.
> — When you accidently notice the sublime.
> — Somersaults and duels.
> — Another day when you see a woman with really red hair. I mean really red hair.
> — A wedding day.
> — A plain day.
> — So we'll try again? Okay?
> — Okay.
> — Okay?
> — Okay.

The balance here between resolution and uncertainty, between the ordinary and the sublime, dramatizes the tension between the instinct for romance and the impulse of antiromance. While not taking the leap, the characters yet keep its possibility alive, draining off their longing and objectifying it at the same time. And the story is self-referential, especially if we read the third line here, "Somersaults and duels," as a metaphor for both the sublime and the dialogue form. The cosmos and the experience of the sublime have often been imagined as a *concordia discors*, a balancing dialectic of opposites, a sort of dynamic equilibrium, and the same is true for dialogue and drama. And somersaults and duels are appropriate images, respectively, of a self-enclosing action and a two-in-oneness, so that the onward push of the story, which ends in stasis, is clearly represented. And the tension between a wedding day and a plain day stands for the experience of a religious conversion where the marvelous and the ordinary are somehow transformed into one another. The story's form allows it to show, as it were, what it can't show, and to close on that very gesture that it is unable to make. The story's deepest irony is that it "represents" the structure of a leap of faith even as it "misrepresents" its characters' ability to make such a leap.

We find a similar play with forms of representation in "Robert Kennedy Saved From Drowning," to return to that story briefly, and to discuss Barthelme's use of romance. Parody and romance may be thought of as opposite ends of the spectrum of representation. Romance equates the wish with the fact; parody keeps us always aware of their separation. Parody enacts a form of antiromance, in that it offers us a desirable style or content while at the same time withholding its total acceptance. Barthelme ends the Kennedy story with a scene in which K. is prefigured as either Zorro or a romance knight, complete with mock-chivalric equipment. (Ironically, the equipment is also that of a magician, another romance figure.) The author, or rather the story's authorial voice is given a chance to save K., and we can see in this episode the allegory of a sort of redemption of fictional consciousness. For what the author is saving is less an individual than the center of his own story, the excuse of his fictionmaking. The actual events of the incident represent the ultimate fantasy of sorts, for the little man has a chance to save the hero. But the hero's response indicates that the redeeming act results only in an everyday occurrence, and so the realm of romance is shattered as soon as it's realized. The reality principle, the condescension of heroes, quickly and unspectacularly replaces the pleasure principle, in which the author both creates and empowers heroes. The ironist here is in fact saving himself from drowning, by creating an object with powers to represent both the world of dreams and the world of fact.

K. Saved from Drowning

K. in the water. His flat black hat, his black cape, his sword are on the shore. He retains his mask. His hands beat the surface of the water which tears and rips about him. The white foam, the green depths. I throw a line, the coils leaping out over the surface of the water. He has missed it. No, it appears that he has it. His right hand (sword arm) grasps the line that I have thrown him. I am on the bank, the rope wound round my waist, braced against a rock. K. now has both hands on the line. I pull him out of the water. He stands now on the bank, gasping.

"Thank you."

*   *   *

This might be the place to offer a tentative typology[10] of Barthelme's fiction. As the first chapter suggested, a variety of formal inventiveness is one of the hallmarks of these stories. Keeping this in mind, we can nevertheless suggest five categories into which a large portion of the stories fit. These categories are not meant to be rigid, and indeed several stories could easily fit into more than one. However, I think the categories show that Barthelme does have a fairly coherent poetics of fiction, and that his inventiveness is not

10. See also David Lodge, *The Modes of Modern Writing* (Ithaca, N.Y.: Cornell University Press, 1977), where a typology of modes in postmodernist fiction is outlined. Lodge includes such devices as discontinuity, short-circuit (exposing conventions while using them), and excess (overloading the text with specificity). My typology is grounded more on structural forms, whereas Lodge tends to focus on local effects of texture and grammar. In the earlier portions of the book he discusses the high-modernist mode by using the concepts of metaphor and metonymy. Though he doesn't say so directly, I think these terms don't work well for a writer like Barthelme, whose style is so various.

purely random or arbitrary.

Total aleatory structure: This is I think the least successful kind of story. Examples would range from "Alice" and "A Picture History of the War" in *Unspeakable Practices*, to "Bone Bubbles" in *City Life*, to "Departures" in *Sadness*. The earliest example is "The Viennese Opera Ball" from *Come Back, Dr. Caligari*. In such stories, Barthelme is using surreal juxtaposition almost exclusively. Everything is surface, there is little or no silhouetting since it is hard to distinguish background structure from foreground detail, or inner form from outer reality. These stories demonstrate Barthelme's obvious indebtedness to an avant-garde program of radical experimentation. Like the William Carlos Williams of *Kora in Hell* and the John Ashbery of *The Tennis Court Oath*, Barthelme evidently felt the need to go all the way into incoherence before he could clearly define the limits of his art.

The surreal place: Here the clearest examples are "City Life" from the volume of that name, and "Paraguay" and "At the Tolstoy Museum" from the same collection. "The Flight of Pigeons from the Palace" in *Sadness* is a special case in this category. This group has obvious affinities to the aesthetic utopias, and dystopias, created by other writers such as Vonnegut (his Tramalfador), Borges (his "Tlön, Uqbar, Orbis Tertius"), and Brautigan. In the broadest sense these are versions, and sometimes parodies, of Baudelaire's endless beyond, the realm of *"luxe calme et volupte."* Barthelme is drawn to such places not only because of his surrealist predilections, but also because of his attraction to the realm of romance. "What a happy time that was, when all the electricity went away! If only we could recreate that paradise!" says one of the characters in "City Life," a picture of urban dystopia. "The Flight of Pigeons" is about an entertainment show that is enacted in the "noble and empty spaces" of an abandoned palace. The strain and improbability of maintaining a constant supply of wonders becomes the story's main point, suggesting that the realm of romance is destined for foreclosure.

The counterpointed plot: This is a structure Barthelme uses partially in many cases, though the clearest examples would be stories like "Views of My Father Weeping," from *City Life*, and "The Catechist," from *Sadness*. In this second story, two priests meet and have the same conversation every day, in which "no detail changes." The narrator-priest is apparently having an affair with a woman he meets in a park, where there are guards who are abusing a group of mothers. The catechist-priest reads aloud to the narrator from the catechism and other accounts, including a Reuters news item, about various aspects of Catholic ritual. At one level the story parodies the inadequacy of the catechetical structure in dealing with the narrator's difficulties. At another level, the catechist does deal with the narrator's situation (at least as directly as the narrator himself), but does so tangentially, elliptically, accepting the narrator's offense against church law and yet questioning his sincerity and motivation. The guard's abuse of the mothers stands as a sort of metaphor for both plots—the adultery and the catechism lesson—since it conveys a situation that ought to call forth decisive action but has instead produced a routinized ineffectiveness. (The narrator writes letters of complaint about the abuse, but to no avail.) Other stories that use counterpointed plots often do so in such a way that the plots comment on each other. But often the situations in each plot revolve around stymied characters, so instead of one plot "clarifying" another, we get instead a sort of twinned puzzle, in which neither plot is resolvable. Also this structure occurs in stories where the ostensible situation is counterpointed by the main character's guilt or secret longings, as in "The Indian Uprising" from *Unspeakable Practices*, where the social revolution is set against the narrator's rather juvenile love fantasies. The double-mindedness, the radical ambiguity of Barthelme's vision is clearly apparent in such structures.

The extended conceit: This category shows Barthelme at his most playful, as he elaborately and parodically extends some central figure. This extension is itself a form of doubleness, as it often de-creates its own structure by a kind of *reductio ad absurdum* and at the same time vindicates the surreal logic that first generated the conceit. In a way, such stories are serious lampoons. Here the clearest examples are "The Balloon"; "The City of Churches" from *Sadness*; "The Police Band" from *Unspeakable Practices*; "The Policeman's Ball" and "On Angels" from *City Life*; and "Some of Us Have Been Threatening Our Friend Colby," "The Reference," and "Porcupines at the University," from *Amateurs*. These stories are often close to the spirit of the pieces in *Guilty Pleasures*, some of which originally appeared unsigned in the "Comment" column of *The New Yorker*. (The novel *The Dead Father* might be read as an extended conceit, in which the question of how to deal with the past is equated with how to dispose of the corpse of the father.) These are divertissements, *jeux d'esprit* designed in large part for the knowing audience who delights as much in skill of execution as in the moral or social insights implicit in the work. But the best of these stories do contain references, sometimes barbed, sometimes veiled, to the various problems that beset modern society. Take "Porcupines at the University," for example. As the title suggests, this threatened invasion of porcupines desiring entrance to higher education can be read simply as a broad satire on a bureaucracy confronted with the unusual and unassimilable. Barthelme plays the comic aspects for all they're worth by also parodying the university administrators as they confront the redneck "wranglers" who are leading the herd of porcupines. The story thus becomes a satire on Eastern administrators versus the local population, as well as a put-down of modern educational malaise, for the Dean's wife suggests the porcupines can all register for a course in "Alternate Life Styles." The wranglers decide not to face down the Dean, who has armed himself with a Gatling gun. Instead they decide to move the herd to New York City, and so it's possible to read the story as a not-so-sly dig at the City University of New York's policy of open admissions, in which any student with a high-school diploma was guaranteed entrance into college. (This at a time when the high schools were graduating many people who could not read or write.) Again, the story parodies both sides: the frantic Dean with his quick resort to brute force and the opportunistic wranglers looking for any solution to their problem.

Some of these extended conceits do have characteristics they share with stories in other categories. "City of Churches," for example, might be seen as a story about a "surreal place," but I think it is more obviously a conceit about the proliferation of ecclesiastical structures and rabid real-estate developers in certain Midwestern American cities. Likewise with "The Reference," in which one Mr. McPartland has listed several people as references on his application, and the story consists of a phone conversation in which one reference is "checked out." The specific referee in the story lives in Arkansas, so Barthelme is able to satirize not only job requirements but also the local culture of Arkansas. But this particular category does show quite clearly Barthelme's fascination with the problems of structure and closure, as the conceit has to be handled with just the right mix of diligence and insouciance.

Parodies of narrative structure: This category would be the largest and most various if we included partial examples. But the purest examples would be "Florence Green is 81" and "Me and Miss Mandible," from *Come Back, Dr. Caligari*, both of which parody the unreliable narrator; "Sentence," from *City Life*, which is one long sentence starting with "or" and ending without a period, thus ironically undercutting the closure of traditional grammar and narrative form and playing with the pun on "sentence" (grammatical unit and prescribed term of punishment); "Concerning the Bodyguard," from *Great Days*, which is made up almost entirely of rhetorical questions such as a reader would likely ask of a story; and "The Sandman," from *Sadness*, a story in the form of a letter addressed to the narrator's girlfriend's psychiatrist. Each of these examples takes a traditional element of narration and subjects it to some sort of distortion, usually involving self-referentiality. "Florence Green is 81," for example, has this passage:

> . . . we have roles to play, thou and I: you are the doctor
> (washing your hands between hours), and I, I am, I think, the
> nervous dreary patient. I am free associating, brilliantly, bril-
> liantly, to put you into the problem.

The language at one point ("thou and I") would suggest a
familar letter of the eighteenth century, while the rest of the
passage clearly indicates an analysand talking to his psychiatrist. The story plays and replays varied motifs, mimicking the free-association method and yet also implying
that the entire performance is planned with cunning attention ("we have roles to play"). Nowhere is the implicit
questioning of the self-analytic frame of mind, with all the
bedeviled trappings of "therapeutic man," more evident in
Barthelme's work than in this story (one of his earliest, by
the way). And this is achieved in large measure by the
blurring of the narrative frame: do we have a personal letter
to a friend, or a session between patient and doctor, or a
direct address by a deranged narrator to us, the readers?
Some might think the three frame-situations are similar
enough to begin with, so their confusion by the narrator
doesn't signify anything of importance. Yet by placing them
together while at the same time disjoining them (a strategy
realized by the parodic mode), we see what a tangle of false
sincerity and questionable self-presentation is involved in
each. The entrapping structure of each social situation is
both reflected and called into question by the play with
narrative structure. From the beginning, I would argue,
Barthelme was using parody for purposes that were in part
serious.

And this brings us back once again to the question of the
"anxious object." For Barthelme it is narrative structures
themselves which have the most unclear status. Is the
narrative structure, in the eyes of the post-modern artist,
the quintessential piece of junk, since so often these structures rest on assumptions about individual psychology,
linear time, and social order that are by and large hopelessly
out of date? But nowhere does Barthelme's fiction wholly
reject or wholly assent to the contemporary world. The

world is always subject in these stories to an endless figuration, to unceasing impulses toward romance and fantasy. So if narrative doesn't adequately or accurately reflect the world, it doesn't bow down before it either. Rather it urges the world to confess its guilty pleasures, to admit between the hourly handwashings that it is in love with brillance and dazzlement. And what better way to demonstrate this self-denying, self-fulfilling love than to fix on those broken bits of tales and information that manage to preserve the traces of our desire?

IV. CONCLUSION

I should begin this conclusion with the usual disclaimer
that it is hard to summarize the works of a writer as protean
as Barthelme. In this case the usual disclaimer has more
than the usual truth. But I will try nevertheless to make
something like conclusive statements on the more than one
hundred stories Barthelme has published. First some reflections on his career. Some of the stories in his first collection,
especially "Me and Miss Mandible" and "Florence Green is
81," are as skillful as any of the others he published in the
subsequent twenty years. Barthelme's skill has never been
doubted, and it developed very early, as is sometimes the
case with certain forms of mimicry. So the question of
growth becomes cloudy in his case, and his techniques of
collage and parody have rather expanded in their application than deepened in their profundity. Though he has not
"grown" from book to book, and allowing for the soft focus
of generalization, Barthelme's movement can nevertheless
be sketched.

In his third book of stories, *City Life*, Barthelme pushed
the limits of traditional narrative further than he had in his
first two. In *City Life* we get the first stories to use line
engravings, for example. And the play with ideas in "On
Angels" and "Kierkegaard Unfair to Schlegel" made the use
of abstract philosophical arguments more apparent. *City
Life* is perhaps the most experimental of Barthelme's books.[1]
Almost no story in it has a completely "normal" typographical surface. Of course such typographical innovations are no guarantee that the narrative is equally non-
traditional, but in this case the link is fairly certain. And for

1. See the discussion by Morris Dickstein, in *The Gates of Eden: American
Culture in the Sixties* (New York: Basic Books, 1977), pp. 218–26. Here *City
Life* is praised as the most demanding and rewarding of Barthelme's collec-
tions, a book with "new risks and new emotional defeats, [that] represents
a quite different sort of fictional victory," different from *Snow White* and
Sadness and the work of many other experimental fictionists.

Sixty Stories Barthelme has retained nine out of fourteen of the stories from *City Life*, the highest proportion of all the books in this regard. (The low is from the earliest, *Come Back, Dr. Caligari*, where only four of fourteen are reprinted. The highest total number is from the most recent collection, *Great Days*, where ten of sixteen are used. This may indicate how the topicality of references in the stories reduces their durability.) But in no other volume, with the exception of *Guilty Pleasures*, is the surface and structure of so many stories more clearly innovative than in *City Life*.

With *Sadness* and *Amateurs* Barthelme seemed to have retreated somewhat from the aggressive innovations of *City Life*. There are several stories in these two later volumes that are especially melancholic, focusing rather with an air of desperation on characters stymied by their circumstances. "Critique de la Vie Quotidienne," from *Sadness*, is the best example of this. In fact *Sadness* lives up to its title, for I think it is the volume with the least amount of playful buffoonery. *Amateurs*, which appeared four years after *Sadness*, returns in part to the sense of whackiness that was a staple in the earlier volumes. Stories from *Amateurs* like "Porcupines at the University" and "The Reference" show Barthelme at his wittiest, though a passage from the latter seems to speak meaningfully out of context: "Different folk I talk to in different ways. I got to keep myself interested." Some of the stories in these two volumes seem slight, coming close to the level of a mere exercise; here I would list "The Educational Experience" and "The Wound" from *Amateurs* as examples, neither of which is included in *Sixty Stories*.

Of all the volumes, I find *Great Days* the least satisfying as a whole. In its defense I would say its humor is especially "smart," though this is a quality that is present in most of the stories, so it's hard to be precise as to why this book seems especially marked by it. But "Cortes and Montezuma" and "The King of Jazz" seem to me to be addressed to a very small audience. With a writer like Barthelme, who clearly doesn't address the general reader in the first place, this might not seem like a handicap. But the seriousness of the stories is sacrificed to their structure. The ending of "The Leap," for example, with its self-referential "somersaults and duels," is part of this. But also the strictly dialogue stories, of which there are seven, serve to focus attention on the implicit challenge that each Barthelme story presents, a challenge to his skills and our quickness and patience. To use that tried but true formula, this is not the book of his I would urge a new reader to begin with (for me that book would be *Amateurs* or *Sadness*).

In short, Barthelme may have developed his talent as far as is possible, though obviously such predictions are always tentative. In *Snow White* and *The Dead Father*, he has little more than indicated that he wants to write a novel, for these books are merely extensions of a style that works better in the short-story form. Of course one of the corollaries of my argument is that Barthelme's vision is fundamentally *not* novelistic. If true, this corollary could be especially burdensome, since further work in the short-story form may come to represent just more of the same for Barthelme, no matter how topical or witty he makes the next story. Barthelme has, as I have tried to show, always been close to several genres, and he may end up as a representative of the most insubstantial of all: the chronicle of fashion. So far, I think, his work has been daring enough to grapple with the mundane and transitory without being swamped by it. But as Auden suggested by the very title of his book of criticism, *The Dyer's Hand*, any artist is bound to be stained by the colors of whatever palette he chooses to work with.

Northrop Frye, in his *Anatomy of Criticism*, has discussed the ironic mode in fiction as that where the author is of a higher order of consciousness than his characters. Barthelme fits this description well at first glance. But what, exactly, does he see, and what, if anything, does his authorial freedom allow him that is denied to his characters? Surely his characters are limited, neurotic victims of overdetermined behavior and oversensitized consciousness. But does Barthelme, like Joyce for example, have a belief in the transcendent, universalizing power of art? Does he, like

Doris Lessing, have a meliorist if not utopian view of civilization? To shift the terms around, does he suffer from a convincing sense of the evil of banality, as some find in Beckett? Does he have a sense of the problem of ethnic destiny, such as Philip Roth continues to address? The implicit answer in each case is no, and this is what makes Barthelme less than a major writer for many readers. But viewed from another vantage point—to invoke his own double-mindedness—it is this very absence of a central philosophical, historical, or metaphysical given that makes Barthelme an important if not a major writer.

He is perhaps the final post-Enlightenment writer, the final skeptic, the last wing beat of Minerva's owl. At his most trenchant, which is often his most funny, Barthelme exhibits a hyperconsciousness that seems to double its own double-mindedness into a glut of parodic contexts. Earlier I mentioned the concept of rationalization as one of the chief subjects of Barthelme's attention. He addresses this subject directly in a paragraph from the story "Paraguay," and "applies" the process to that chief reservoir of the irrational, art itself. What we see here is Weber's notion satirized by exaggeration, and yet the mad logic of the situation manages to convey a discomfiting set of truths about the production of commodified art in a world of fads, media exposure, the celebrity status of writers, the whirl of government and foundation grants and awards committees—the whole "product mix" of the contemporary scene.

> *Rationalization* The problems of art. New artists have been obtained. These do not object to, and indeed argue enthusiastically for, the rationalization process. Production is up. Quality-control devices have been installed at those points where the interests of artists and audience intersect. Shipping and distribution have been improved out of all recognition. (It is in this area, they say in Paraguay, that traditional practices were most blameworthy.) The rationalized art is dispatched from central art dumps to regional art dumps, and from there into the lifestreams of cities. Each citizen is given as much art as his system can tolerate. Marketing considerations have not been allowed to dictate product mix; rather, each artist is encouraged to maintain, in his software, highly personal,

even idiosyncratic, standards (the so-called "hand of the artist" concept). Rationalization produces simpler circuits and, therefore, a saving in hardware. Each artist's product is translated into a statement in symbolic logic. The statement is then "minimized" by various clever methods. The simpler statement is translated back into the design of a simpler circuit. Foamed by a number of techniques, the art is then run through heavy steel rollers. Flip-flop switches control its further development. Sheet art is generally dried in smoke and is dark brown in color. Bulk art is air-dried, and changes color in particular historical epochs.

Perhaps the most telling irony here is the inclusion of a desire to maintain a belief in "highly personal, even idiosyncratic, standards" in the midst of relentless standardization. Barthelme's uncanny ability to include just those contradictory, yet thoroughly plausible and "realistic," points of the typical bureaucratic thought process is one of the best measures of his skill as a writer. His mimicry of the rationalized and rationalizing language is quite funny, even down to the little twist of referring to the concept of individual standards as "so-called." And critics, myself included, can hardly be comfortable when they realize who is the object of the irony implicit in categorizing art into "sheet" and "bulk" forms, complete with color coding. A writer who can write with this many levels of irony has incorporated a great deal of critical energy into his work. This passage alone would prove that Barthelme has already entered into a very complex stage of consciousness, a stage, as Erich Heller puts it, "where every act of creation is inseparable from the critique of its medium, and every work, intensely reflecting upon itself, looks like the embodied doubt of its own possibility."[2]

The figure of the artist plays a crucial role in Barthelme's work, from such broad satire as "The Dolt" to the Paul Klee story, from such subtle stories as "Daumier" to the harsh tones of "The Death of Edward Lear" ("People who had attended the death of Edward Lear agreed that, all in all, it

2. In *The Artist's Journey Into The Interior* (New York: Random House, 1968), p. 226.

had been a somewhat tedious performance"). I would say the three chief subjects of Barthelme's fiction are the futility of work in a post-industrial society, the emotional disorientation of divorce (in both literal and metaphoric terms), and the impotent double-mindedness of the artist. Of these three, the third is perhaps the most ironic and subject to the most complex forms of parodic layering of contexts and contradictions. A consideration of one of his best stories on this subject can serve as a concluding occasion to explore some of Barthelme's most challenging ideas. It is in "Daumier," from *Sadness*, that I think Barthelme comes closest to his most important story. It is also where he comes closest to showing his hand, as it were, about the very problem of representation in a world of insatiable selves driven by the desire for things that turn to junk even as they become the symbols of satisfied need.

Ostensibly "Daumier" is an example of the counterpointed plot. The narrative voice of the story, a self-conscious writer who reveals little direct information about his situation, dominates the enveloping plot. The story inside the story concerns the writer's created character, named Daumier and identified as a surrogate of the author, and his totally absurd adventures. These adventures involve a parody of the Dumas tale of the three musketeers, here called (or "played by") Daumier and his two associates, Mr. Bellows and Mr. Hawkins. Actually the parody of Dumas is rather briefly mentioned, and the three men are more occupied with their improbable mission, to escort fifteen hundred *au pair* girls to safety away from a band of marauding Jesuits. Their mission fails, and the narrative is flitly presented, with the plot given in summary form and the crisis treated like the ruse of a Saturday afternoon Western. But the chief connections between the two plots are what give the story its interest. The narrative voice clearly announces the theme of the story as well as its "solution." The self is insatiable, "a dirty great villain," and it must be taught control and humility by its own surrogates. The surrogate "is in principle satiable," and so Daumier is created to "know his limits." But of course the surrogate becomes as equally insatiable as any other self, and indeed the story ends with Celeste, Daumier's girl friend in the absurd inner plot, becoming the object of the narrator's love. In the meantime, Amelia, the narrator's "real" lover, continues to live with him. The story concludes by deliberately confusing Amelia and Celeste—both are making a *daube* by putting "strips of optional pork in the bottom of a pot"—so that, as in a Renaissance masque, the line between artifice and reality is deliberately blurred. The narrator even shows us his dissembling, as he announces that he will wrap his characters in tissue paper and put them away until some day when again his "soul is sickly and full of sores." So the principle of surrogation, as the narrator dispassionately calls it, works and doesn't work. The surrogate self not only becomes insatiable, but it can be tolerated only so long as it supplies the "original" self with some form of real or imagined satisfaction. Barthelme has dramatized in a very funny, indeed ridiculous, way the Nietzschean notion that art is what we have to keep us from perishing from the truth.

Several aspects of the story's tone convey important variations on this central theme. The story we tell ourselves, after we're aware that all stories are equally false, and equally true projections of an insatiable ego, hardly matters. True, this "final" story contains elements that recur: an outside threat, sublimated desire and reversal (Celeste is, of course, one of the *au pair* girls Daumier is supposed to be protecting), ambiguity of motive, heroic self-doubt, and so forth. But all stories are equally preposterous (a herd of *au pair* girls) and grounded in some sense of historical verifiability (the story gives the dates of the expulsion of the Jesuits from various European countries). And, perhaps most important, the characters in a story are always surrogates of the narrator, or the narrator's view of his audience's character, and so Daumier discovers—can only discover—what his narrator conceives as the answer to *his* dilemma.

This discovery, as you might expect, is a form of double-mindedness. First there is the insatiability of the self. Then there is the complementary, paradoxical truth that "You must fight against the cocoon of habituation which covers everything, if you let it." We can never be satisfied; we must always avoid satisfaction.

Pinched between these two contradictory truths is the very appetite that ensures the truth of both. Throughout the story images of food recur, and the penultimate paragraph describes a meal that Daumier (or the narrator; at this point the two are indistinguishable) has prepared for Celeste. It is Barthelme's humor at its broadest, but it also conveys how desire recycles the junk of a fallen world and, given the right self-delusion and the right self-control, turns junk into the food of the gods. We recall Flaubert's great injunction for the autonomous artist trapped in the nets of history: "Dress like a bourgeois and think like a demi-god." Barthelme tops off his junk-food feast of Fritos and Planters Nuts and onion dip with "generous amounts of Tab, a fiery liquor brewed under license by the Coca-Cola Company which will not divulge the age-old secret recipe no matter how one begs and pleads with them but yearly allows a small quantity to circulate to certain connoisseurs and bibbers whose credentials meet the very rigid requirements of the Cellar-master." Ironically, of course, we realize that Tab probably is "brewed" with the same sedulous care given rare whisky, at least as that care is embodied in the latest technology and "quality control." And who is enough of an anti-utilitarian to deny the Coca-Cola Company its place in the scheme of things? And how can we distinguish imagined satisfaction from "the real thing," for we are satisfied only by what we crave, and our cravings are beyond calculation. Celeste looks at the banquet and bluntly asks, "Where is the food?" Daumier can only answer: " 'You do not recognize a meal spiritually prepared,' I said, hurt in the self-love." Only with sufficient self-regard can we provide something for others beyond ourselves. Only relentless desire for the spiritual takes us away from the unrelentingly ordinary.

Such paradoxes at the level of appetite have counterparts at other levels, especially that of the epistemological. Here Barthelme's irony insists that we can know nothing with certainty, that all our faith is prey to double-mindedness, yet we must pursue knowledge at all costs and with absolute honesty. By using Daumier as the main character in this story, Barthelme implicitly says that he himself is like the French painter. And Daumier might briefly be described as an artist who desired to work in the grand style but was driven to satire by the self-defeating wills of the avaricious bourgeois that surrounded him. Barthelme, then, becomes the epitome of the petit bourgeois, one who must exploit his own labor, neither owner nor worker, but someone always torn between the absolutes of "yes" and "no." Barthes has described this mental state as "Neither-Norism." With Barthelme, however, his artist figures often want "*both* this *and* that," a paradox of desire, while they know they can affirm "*neither* this *nor* that" with unflagging commitment, a paradox of knowledge. For Barthes, "neither-norism" is a way of defusing desire, of managing an otherwise unknowable world. It is what Barthelme's characters sometimes descend to, what they are often threatened with, and what the author himself is always confronting. Here is Barthes's description of the mental maneuver:

> *Neither-Norism.* By this I mean this mythological figure which consists in stating two opposites and balancing the one by the other so as to reject them both. (I want *neither* this *nor* that.) It is on the whole a bourgeois figure, for it relates to a modern form of liberalism. We find again here the figure of the scales: reality is first reduced to analogues; then it is weighed; finally, equality having been ascertained, it is got rid of. Here also there is magical behaviour: both parties are dismissed because it is embarrassing to choose between them; one flees from an intolerable reality, reducing it to two opposites which balance each other only inasmuch as they are purely formal, relieved of all their specific weight. Neither-Norism can have degraded forms: in astrology, for example, ill-luck is always followed by equal good-luck; they are always predicted in a prudently compensatory perspec-

tive: a final equilibrium immobilizes values, life, destiny, etc.: one no longer needs to choose, but only to endorse.[3]

The opposites in Barthelme's paradox, "inasmuch as they are purely formal," leave him in a stranded position, with no Archimedean point of moral criticism.

Unless of course we say that for Barthelme this point is the very junkiness of the world. By constantly reimmersing himself in the world of junk and fragments, Barthelme achieves a *sort* of resolution. We can even see this as a revenge of sorts against the condition about which Henry James first complained: American fiction writers have no stable signs of social reality. In a society committed to change and upward mobility the only recourse for writers is to create some form of romance, even if it is based on failed desires, with only junk as the signs of reality. Barthelme's double-mindedness suggests that there are only desires and fantasies, and they are never to be satisfied.

Finally, there are at least two ways to aestheticize junk and fragments, to make them safe for literature. The first would treat them as "Notes toward a unity." This approach comes from too much desire for organic wholeness, a Coleridgean *hubris* that always delays closure or revelation since the secret is too great. The second treats them as "Passages from a lost original." This is the route of nostalgia, the constant recall of a consistently vanished plenitude. Barthelme's art refuses to devote itself exclusively to either of these assumptions, nor to deny either. Barthelme is saved from drowning in a world of fragments by his ironic manipulation of them. And he is saved from drowning in his own irony by a commitment to those fragments as the saving reality. He does this by sacrificing any consistently inward feeling of a final truth. But he never lets us forget how the absence of such a truth feels. And from *that*, we can almost see the truth for ourselves.

3. *Mythologies*, trans. Annette Lavers (New York: Hill & Wang, 1972), p. 153.